grace

from the

garden

grace

from the

garden

changing the world
one garden at a time

debra landwehr engle

RODALE

© 2003 by Debra Landwehr Engle
Cover photograph © Francesca Yorke/Taxi
Interior photograph © Rodale Images

Printed in the United States of America
Rodale Inc. makes every effort to use acid-free ∞ , recycled paper ♻ .

Book design by Joanna Williams

Library of Congress Cataloging-in-Publication Data

Engle, Debra Landwehr.
    Grace from the garden : changing the world one garden at a
time / Debra Landwehr Engle.
        p.   cm.
    ISBN 1–57954–685–4 hardcover
    1. Gardeners—United States—Anecdotes.   2. Gardening—Uni-
ted States—Anecdotes.   3. Gardens—United States—Anecdotes.
I. Title.
SB455.E75 2003
635—dc21   2002155033

Distributed to the book trade by St. Martin's Press

2   4   6   8   10   9   7   5   3   1   hardcover

Visit us on the Web at www.rodalestore.com, or call us toll-free at
(800) 848-4735.

WE **INSPIRE** AND **ENABLE** PEOPLE TO IMPROVE
THEIR LIVES AND THE WORLD AROUND THEM

❧❧❧

To my parents, Burton and Clara Landwehr,
for always cultivating with love

acknowledgments

For helping to plant the seeds of this book, I'm grateful to LuAnn Brandsen, editor of *Country Gardens* magazine, whose own life is a model of the positive role gardeners play in the world. Literary agents Jo Fagan and Stacey Glick believed in the book from the beginning and saw it through to the end. And my editor at Rodale, Jennifer Kushnier, expertly shepherded this project with unfailing patience and calm.

Countless friends model the many ways in which change can be achieved. They provide daily support and encouragement, understanding the need to witness miracles and tell about them. A special thanks to Pam Schoffner and Julie Janss for reviving our writers' group and offering thoughtful feedback as the book developed.

During the writing of the book, I spent two weeks at Goucher College, beginning my work toward a master's degree in creative nonfiction writing. Thank you to my mentor, Lisa Knopp, and the students in my small group for their encouragement and insights on early chapters.

I am grateful for an extended family that is eminently respectful and steadfast. I couldn't have done this project without Bob, my partner in life, who always looks at the solution instead of the problem. With graciousness, love, and wisdom, he assisted with interviews, fashioned a writing table for the van so I could work as we traveled, and made kettle corn at the most opportune time.

Finally, a special thanks to all the people who agreed to share their stories for this book. In every way, gardeners bring a bit of heaven to earth.

*The telling question of a person's life
is their relationship to the infinite.*
—*Carl Jung*

c o n t e n t s

introduction ❧ *xi*

gardens that teach ❧ 1
good questions ❧ *7*
wild one ❧ *21*
interplanting ❧ *34*

gardens that nourish ❧ 47
heaven and earth ❧ *53*
greetings from rocky roost ❧ *70*
remembering ❧ *83*

gardens that unite ❧ 95
gardener without borders ❧ *101*
mother tongue ❧ *115*
we the people ❧ *129*

ix

gardens that inspire ∽ 143
market day ∽ *149*
fresh start ∽ *162*
love story ∽ *176*

gardens that heal ∽ 191
truth or dare ∽ *197*
kids matter ∽ *210*
grace from the garden ∽ *221*

appendix: resources ∽ *235*

x

introduction

It's an early June morning in Iowa, a bit hazy and breezy, but warm. I imagine my mom is headed out to her garden right now. She lives in town; I live in the country. But I can almost see her thirty miles away, sitting on the edge of her bed for a few moments, putting her feet in her slippers, and padding out to the garden before bringing in the newspaper or fixing her one cup of coffee.

She has done this as long as I can remember, and now that she's eighty-seven, I marvel at the fact that she can do it at all. It's telling to walk the garden with her, especially in early spring. Green shoots of something will be poking through the ground, and she'll point at them with her toe. "Oh, there are some of your dad's wildflowers," she'll say. "This will be a good spot for them." Or, "Hmm, hollyhocks. How did they get all the way over here?" I stand by and nod in wonder, for I'm still unable to discern one seedling from another.

If my mom moves plants to new locations, she digs them with great care, as if their roots were a baby's limbs, then she pats them into the ground. There are no throwaways here. Each one is treated individually and with reverence, in much the same way that my mom and dad raised their six children.

Thanks to my parents, I've never been far from a garden. I can't say that I appreciated the softball-sized turnips or Big Boy tomatoes my dad grew, especially when the vegetable garden pirated the spot where the swingset sat when we were little. I can't say that I always appreciated my mom's flowers, either, so abundant they were, and so easy to take for granted. I grew up in a world in which I didn't realize that other people had no flowers at all.

But as the seasons of life have passed, I've learned that gardening is about more than putting plants in the ground and watching them grow. It is about all the things my parents taught us and about the gifts that people everywhere are hoping to give beyond their communities.

As I've worked on this book, I've come to realize that people don't use gardens toward fearful ends. Television and video games—those usual suspects of society's ills—can be used for negative messages. Writing and art, too, often are skewed toward darkness instead of light. But the least little effort in a garden produces beauty. We may hybridize a rose and make it bigger or steal its scent, but we don't tend a rose to destroy it. Words, music, and art pass through our minds and belief systems before they take form. Gardens just pass through our fingers.

There are people who know this. I think every gardener must know it on some level. But there are many gardeners who go beyond the land, taking all that enrichment, spirit, and renewal and applying it to other areas of life in which gardening can do immense good in this world.

I first became aware of some of their stories through my work for *Country Gardens* magazine. The editor and I sat in her office several years ago and envisioned a column that would pay tribute to people who make a difference in their communities by gardening. In working on that column, I became aware of how many stories there are—

stories that defy all the negativity and fear with which we're bombarded each day. These people may not need to have their stories told, but we need to hear them.

In many cases, these gardeners started with a simple idea, something anyone could do, and it grew into a project that altered people's lives. They didn't set out to change the world. They just saw a stretch of grass and wanted to fill it or met urban kids who didn't know where food came from and wanted to teach them.

A few of the gardeners in this book are working with complex issues—progressive systems of food production and distribution, for example, or forging bonds among people in multicultural neighborhoods. For others, the activism of gardening is a private pursuit, disclosed through the everyday acts of child rearing and friendship. No matter what the scope of their stories, I've included them here, believing that any act of tending and nurturing invokes change.

This book is in no way meant to be a comprehensive or even representative list of gardeners. These are people I happened to find and who found me, and I'm guessing that for every one of them, there are thousands more. Although their stories vary widely, the gardeners share the same act of courage: They are willing to look at what needs to be changed. Far from blind to the problems we all face, they see brokenness not as a mandate for despair but as an opportunity for greater wholeness. As evidence, they have taken the generosity of nature and spread it around. These people don't tend their gardens. They are extensions of them.

When I visited the gardeners, many apologized for

their beds being imperfect; we have come to think of gardening as performance art. But what sets these gardens apart is not whether they're free of thistles or weeds. Instead, it's that their intent is as earthy and pure as any of the plants growing within them. The kids at the Florence Crittenton Home in Fullerton, California, won't remember if maverick blades of grass infringed on their green peppers. They *will* remember that they won a blue ribbon for their vibrant daisies and coreopsis and that they could never consider themselves valueless from that point on.

My own spiritual study has taught me that the healing of humanity and the earth we inhabit is all this world is for. Yet when we're bombarded each day with news of snipers, abductors, murderers, terrorists, and war, it's easy to forget that acts of aggression and destruction are not the norm. It's more important than ever, I think, to focus on what's right, on ordinary people who reach inward to find a mission, a passion, a purpose, compassion, determination, creativity, generosity, gratitude, forgiveness, and healing. Their stories are ones I want to hear. They're also the stories worth telling.

And so, over the course of a spring and summer, I visited gardeners around the country, observing firsthand the ways in which they tend their plants and nurture the lives of those around them. I've organized their efforts into five categories: gardens that teach, nourish, unite, inspire, and heal. These classifications are necessarily broad, as the efforts of each of the gardeners fulfill all of those functions and more. Because many of the gardeners are involved in projects that could be transferable to other communities, I've included an appendix at the end of the book where you'll find addresses, phone numbers, Web sites, and suggestions for ways in which you can adapt their ideas or learn more about their endeavors.

The gardeners on these pages are ordinary folks, like my mom, patting a seedling into the ground and stepping lightly around the new transplant. They are you and me, they are all of us, and their energy illumines the world.

My mom will be trimming the spirea today or cutting a bouquet of roses and purple wildflowers for the table. She didn't teach her children to be exceptional gardeners. But she and my dad did teach us to be good people. That's what we're here for, nothing else. All we can do is plant seeds wherever we go.

gardens that teach

My friend Marilyn remembers a time when her daughter, Valerie, was four years old. Marilyn was inside the house working and keeping an eye on Val, who was playing out in the flower garden. After a while, Val came into the house, grabbed Marilyn's hand, and started pulling her toward the door. "Mommy," she said, "come out into my wonderful world."

That phrase has stayed with Marilyn for two decades, a time span measured by the fact that Val is now a college graduate. As Marilyn remembers, she followed her daughter into the garden that day and watched her play. Nothing momentous happened, and at the same time, everything did.

"It was a moment of pure joy and discovery," Marilyn says. Her daughter was learning about the beauty of nature, and Marilyn was relearning it, seen through Valerie's eyes.

Certainly there's no end to discovery in the garden, as Gene and Audrey Garcia are learning. Originally from New Mexico, they moved to a twelve-acre farm east of Rockford, Illinois, in 1999. A house and a barn stood alone on the property, and the Garcias had limited experience on the land. Today, however, they milk their own cow, grind wheat for bread, and fill up freezers with meat and the produce from their garden. The farm, which Audrey named Rose of Sharon, has turned out to be the beginning of a lifelong learning situation for the Garcias and their two home-schooled sons, fifteen-year-old Silas and twelve-year-old Amiel.

For a picture of life at Rose of Sharon Farm, consider this: The family purchased a few chickens, then decided they needed some roosters; now they supply eggs for themselves and a family with ten children near Chicago. Silas and Amiel bought sheep to raise for meat, so they found books that taught them the fine points of sheep stewardship. Of course, the family had to have cows, and then a bull to breed them. The cows have calved, and now the Garcias are milking again. They get more milk than they need, but some of the extra will go to their married daughter's baby, the Garcias' first grandchild. The turkeys they ordered took great delight in consuming weeds and now are coveted for Thanksgiving dinners, weighing in at close to thirty pounds apiece. The boys bought a horse for Christmas one year, built a round pen, and Silas is breaking the horse with the help of instructional videos.

The same exponential growth has occurred in the garden. The Garcias started by taking down a chain-link fence and putting in a few beds. Then they added horse manure for mulch, built raised beds, and started composting. They planted watermelon, squash and pumpkins, chives, rhubarb, raspberries, long-leaf parsley, different kinds of lettuce, and spinach. Because they use chili peppers "like salt," Audrey says, half their garden is devoted to peppers and tomatoes, and Gene bought a book on lasagna gardens. Apple, pear, and peach trees grow in the orchard.

And this is only their third year of gardening.

In 2002, they planted fifty pounds of garlic—more than enough to use and sell. A book is teaching them how to raise better herbs, including sage for poultry dishes and cilantro for salsas and salads. Audrey canned more than eighty quarts of tomatoes, along with jams, tomato juice, and spaghetti sauce. The Garcias harvested the equivalent of five large trash bags full of chili peppers, which they roasted, peeled, and froze to last them through the season. "Everybody who comes over gets hooked on it," Audrey says. "They end up asking for it the next time they come."

The Garcias want their home and gardens to be a place of learning and retreat for city friends who can benefit from fruit trees, a slab of fresh-baked bread, and walkways lined with lilies. On occasion, visitors pull weeds and feed them to the turkeys. They might help roast chili peppers. And they can stay as long as they want and help with the garden. The only requirement is that they go to bed when the sun goes down and wake up when the roosters crow and the lambs start to bay.

The sister of a friend came to stay for a couple of weeks. The fresh air and sunshine did her some good, says Audrey. Even folks from New Mexico discover therapeutic benefits at Rose of Sharon Farm. "They relax and pick tomatoes," Audrey says.

It's also becoming a popular stop for home-schooled kids and parents. "The kids go to the zoo, but then they say to their mom, 'We want to come out to a real farm,'" Audrey says. Field trips are already scheduled.

The Garcias figure that people who don't live on farms are missing out, so they invite friends over every Sunday at least, and usually more often. The ten kids in the Chicago family are like nephews and nieces to the Garcias now. And they've been taught so well about the fine points of living off the land that they'll take over the farm for a week at Thanksgiving, when the Garcias go to New Mexico.

Who knew you could do so much on twelve acres? "We're kind of like *Green Acres*," Audrey says. All the time spent drying herbs and canning tomatoes "doesn't seem like work. It makes you more youthful. We get great joy out of it."

Across the country, gardens are used as teaching tools in everything from outdoor classrooms at public schools to programs for children and adult community learners. But learning from the garden is something that happens in any number of ways, as the Garcia family knows.

"We just enjoy working with our hands, working together as a family, and sharing it with others," Audrey says.

Like so many gardeners, they're sharing their wonderful world.

Clearly, they have a lot to teach us.

good
questions

Man masters nature not by force but by understanding.
—Jacob Bronowski

It appears that Will Allen is just doing his work in his own inner-city neighborhood in Milwaukee, Wisconsin, in an area of town where people wouldn't have access to much affordable produce if it weren't for him. It looks like he's working with elementary school kids, getting them excited about earthworms and soil content and planting impatiens for Mother's Day gifts. It looks like he's teaching teenagers responsibility and horticulture by giving them jobs at his retail outlet and greenhouses.

But behind each of those activities are questions that Will is trying to address. They're issues of urban versus rural farming, sustainable agriculture, global food distribution, food security, and organic foods.

Spend a little time with Will, and your mind starts taking you in all sorts of directions, posing unexpected questions like these:

How much money could a person make raising earthworms?

What's tilapia?

Can hydroponics be used to grow something besides bad tomatoes?

Why do more than thirty-five thousand people on earth starve to death every day?

The questions range from the small and personal to the large and global. This is what Will Allen does to you. He prompts you to look at your own life, your own household, at the food you eat, and the food you throw away. Before you know it, your blind spots start to clear up, and you're reluctantly acknowledging that, well, yeah, maybe you *could* make some changes in your life that would be better for the world.

❧

Thirty-five years ago, no one would have predicted that Will Allen would someday be inspiring discussions of the world food supply. He was on the basketball court then, the first black student to play at the University of Miami. After he graduated, he turned pro, guarding Doctor J as a member of the Miami Floridians, then spending three years in Belgium playing ball.

Will traveled a long way from his native Maryland, but something about his upbringing stayed with him. It was farming, spending his childhood with his five brothers and sister, helping his parents raise vegetables, swine, and poultry. This was his introduction to organic gardening, although he didn't know it at the time. The family just spread the livestock manure on the rows of collards and lettuce and didn't think about giving the process a name.

Will, his wife, and their three children moved to Wisconsin, where they bought a one hundred–acre farm, the last piece of rural ground in urban Milwaukee County. He started raising vegetables, and then he needed an outlet to sell them. So, in 1993, he bought a former floral center on two acres, located on a busy street in a low-income area of the city. A zoning variance had given permission for the property, with its retail space and five dilapidated greenhouses, to be bulldozed and replaced with a church. But Will bought it, fixed it up, named it Will's Roadside Market, and used it to market the produce from his farm. That's when the questions he explored grew more complex: "Why don't kids know where food comes from?" and "Is it possible for small farmers to make a living?"

It's fair to say that Will is an anomaly in the community of Milwaukee. This is a part of the country that grew on European immigrants' efforts first in farming, then in manufacturing. And here's Will Allen, an African American from rural Maryland coming to save the day.

On a Saturday morning in May, he's wearing a TOGETHER WE ARE GROWING POWER T-shirt and a Harley Davidson baseball cap. The veins in his biceps stand out, and his face is fleshy and round. He is constantly in motion, fluid like water. Even when he's talking, he's dipping his scooplike hands into the tilapia water in Greenhouse 2 or resting his foot on a spade as he digs into the compost out back.

This steady activity accounts for the fact that he's launched two major programs in the past ten years. The first, Farm-City Link, taught low-income kids how to grow vegetables, plant flowers in their neighborhoods, and share their harvest with neighbors. The second,

Growing Power, is the one that serves as an umbrella for any number of programs, all operated from Will's former Roadside Market. Will is the co-director and on-site manager. His partner, Hope Finkelstein, first had the vision of an organization that would support community gardens. She now lives in Homer, Alaska, where she's started an arm of Growing Power that includes a community garden and weekend workshops.

Today, the once derelict floral center includes a retail grocery, distribution facility, farmers market, greenhouses, experimental laboratories, training center, and commercial processing kitchen, all rolled into one. In the acre of demonstration gardens out back, hens walk along the grass in "chicken tractors," free-range cages that move with them as they roam, protecting them from predators. They're out there hunting and pecking, right next to the rows of spinach, peas, tomatoes, watermelon, sweet corn, salad mix, okra, and sweet potatoes.

It looks unassuming enough, but the programs going on here could spur debate on everything from the effects of TV on kids to the international politics of biotechnology. And all Will really wants to do is make sure everybody gets a decent meal.

❧

On a typical Monday night, children age eight to thirteen start to run into Greenhouse 1, then stop themselves and slow to a walk. Wearing T-shirts and athletic shoes, they're here from the Boys and Girls Clubs, and they're ready to spend the evening. They're chatty, but they speak in respectful voices, and they do not run—two things on which Will insists. Within those rules, though, they're encouraged to sink their hands into soil, play with the earthworms, and eat a good meal.

Will commands instant respect, but it's not because the kids are afraid of him, even if he does loom over them like a giant. His energy is gentle, instantly comforting. No wonder kids walk into the greenhouses, roll their heads back to look up into his face, and see in it a new way of life.

Growing Power created this children's program for two reasons: because these kids have never seen a seed or what it's capable of, and because a lot of them don't get decent food. Their main meal may be lunch at school; if they're getting a government-subsidized lunch, it costs seventeen cents apiece. Will's not convinced you can feed a kid for seventeen cents. So for the Monday night meals, sponsored by an American Cancer Society grant, Growing Power pays a bit more and gives the kids fresh fruits and vegetables that they actually eat. By the end of the summer, they're eating food they grew themselves.

"Everybody is welcome here," Will says. "Everyone has value, so I try to make sure everybody has a place at the table."

The kids work at a long table, surrounded by pots of geraniums and collards and big mobiles of butterflies. On any particular Monday night, they may be potting plants, transplanting seedlings, or mixing soil.

"All the kids want to come," Will says, and they conform to the rules. "When somebody's talking, everyone listens."

The kids' favorite activity in the greenhouses, next to playing with the rabbits and sticking their hands in the bubbling water of the tilapia tanks, is working with the earthworms. There are millions of them in Greenhouse 2, all munching away on sweet potatoes and corncobs in big wooden boxes covered with burlap bags. The worms are processing the garbage. *Whoops*, Will says, it's not garbage, because none of it goes to waste. The worms wriggle into the middle of those sweet potatoes and send it all through their slithery little bodies, and what comes out the other end are nutrient-rich castings.

The castings are blended with perlite, peat moss, and compost for what Will calls the best soil in the world. He teaches this recipe to the children on Monday nights, and to other kids who come for tours and classes. They also learn that worms eat waste and microorganisms. "I make them repeat it a gazillion times while they're here," Will says. "But they get it."

Castings are the organic farmer's friend, but they could benefit traditional farmers, too—not just as fertilizer but as income. They sell for $1.50 a pound wholesale. Will estimates that there are five thousand pounds of worm castings being produced in Greenhouse 2 right now, and they can be turned over every two months. That's a whopping $45,000 a year, and somebody with a few boxes and burlap bags could do the same and sell the castings as a crop.

I'm thinking they could help save southern Iowa, which, despite being part of the world's breadbasket, has a lot of crummy soil. It also has little industry, few natural attractions, and several proud but deteriorating towns. And if earthworms could help southern Iowa, what could they do in other parts of the world?

The questions continue to surface. Will hasn't voiced them, but they're there, as plain as the tanks of tilapia and the troughs of hydroponic plants and the rabbits and the chickens and the compost. Something else is plain to see, as well: Food shouldn't go to waste. And neither should kids.

"It all starts with food," Will says. "The kids tell me that if they have a good meal, they learn better and they aren't angry. The *kids* tell me that."

If they know it, why doesn't everybody?

❧

So here's an interesting question: Why does an elderly woman who lives not far from Growing Power want to shut down the whole operation?

Growing Power is bordered by a military outpost on one side, commercial buildings on the other, a busy thoroughfare out front, and modest homes in the back. The woman, who lives behind the property, is recovering from surgery, and she has called her alderman to complain. It seems that Will's roosters wake her up in the morning, and she's convinced that Will should be evicted right along with his livestock. 13

Don Richards, the Ninth District alderman, has a plan. He is aware that Growing Power is considered by many townspeople to be subversive. He's going to bring the woman to the greenhouses so Will can give her a tour, and maybe then the roosters' crows won't be so annoying.

But crowing roosters aren't the only local opposition Will faces. People don't know what's going on inside those greenhouses, Don says. They don't know, for instance, that by putting teenagers to work in his Teen Youth Corps, training them in everything from retail sales to horticulture and offering them a chance at college scholarships, Will is redirecting kids who might have been breaking into neighborhood houses.

And then there's the continuing issue of zoning. Some of the neighbors still want to tear down Growing Power and build a church. As a former priest, Alderman Richards has an answer for them: Matthew 31:35. ". . . for I was hungry and you gave me food, I was thirsty and you gave me drink, I was a stranger and you welcomed me . . ."

"In that sense," he says, "this is a church."

◦◗◦

On this Saturday morning, it seems peaceful enough at Growing Power, even though a steady stream of people are in and out of Growing Power's retail grocery space up front, where bowls and baskets hold fresh produce for sale. Shelves offer syrup, honey, fig preserves, molasses, pork brains, beef tripe, hot sauce, chow-chow relish, and frozen lima beans, in keeping with Will's idea to make regional food available for people who move from the South and can't get it anywhere else.

This is also the place where local residents come to buy their Market Baskets, a centerpiece of the Growing Power program. In the past two days, two hundred Market Baskets (actually paper sacks) have been purchased, mostly by people in the neighborhood. When Will starts pulling out produce to show me the quality of what's inside, the sack seems bottomless. One bag holds lettuce, grapefruit, bananas, apples, peppers, broccoli, cabbage, corn, cucumbers, carrots, sweet potatoes, an orange and onion, a potato, and honey. For Mother's Day, the Growing Power staff will add eggs and a small pot of impatiens. All for twelve dollars, which is about half the cost of what consumers would pay in an area grocery store.

"I want everybody to have access to affordable food," Will says.

The pesticide-free produce comes from all over the country through the Rainbow Farmer's Cooperative, a network of small farms. The Market Basket distribution system gives the farmers what they need to sustain their business: a regular outlet for their goods and reliable cash income.

Will considers it a success that he can sell the shipped produce through Growing Power in Milwaukee. He would consider it a greater success, though, if small farmers could sell their produce at home, through community food centers in their own neighborhoods and towns.

❧

One of Will's biggest goals is to help communities grow and market their own food, so people can buy produce that was harvested that day. In LaSalle County, Illinois, Will and his staff turned a ten-acre weedy area into a rural farm with the help of homeless men who spent four days a week at the farm and one day in Chicago learning computer skills. In the first growing season, the land produced between five and seven thousand pounds of produce, which were distributed through Growing Power. The experience gave the men needed job skills. "The organization is using agriculture as a way of getting people back in the mainstream," Will says.

In Will's mind, though, farms don't have to be bordered by gravel roads and prairie land. His own one hundred metropolitan acres prove that cultivated land can neighbor coffee shops, high-rise office complexes, car dealerships, or discount centers—anywhere that a plot of land can be cleaned of pollutants and conditioned.

In Chicago alone, he says, seventy thousand unpaved lots, the equivalent of thirty-three square miles, lay vacant. A lot of them are places where houses were taken down, and the soil needs remediation. "With a pickax, it doesn't take long to find out what's in there," he says.

Will is working with the city of Chicago to introduce urban farms in some of those lots. To get the project under way, Growing Power worked with First Presbyterian Church of Chicago, which owns twenty-seven contiguous lots on the south side of the city. Will and his staff installed gardens in four of the lots and will assist in maintaining the land.

From those vacant lots, things turn global fast. Will offers weekend seminars to people from all over the world who come to learn how to start urban farms and Market Basket programs in their own communities. Participants, including farmers, representatives from food-related non-profit groups, businesspeople, government workers, activists, restaurateurs, and others, don't sit around listening to lectures. Will gets them up and around the greenhouses, where they learn how to build small-scale compost systems, construct a worm bin, use vermicompost (worm castings) as an income source, develop an action plan for a community food center or soil remediation, plant and maintain their gardens, and determine strategies for merchandising and marketing their products.

The hope is that they'll return home with much of

the information and skills they need to work with others in their communities, passing along what they've learned as they build community food centers of their own, and linking those centers with the people who can provide the produce they need. It's a holistic system, and nutritious food is at the core of it.

"If you're eating healthy food," Will says, "you won't go to the doctor as much, and you'll have healthy young people."

Which brings up another question:

What if, he wonders, people spent less time watching TV and more time growing and preparing food?

∽

Will's goal is "not to replace farming as we know it, but to enhance it," he says. To find out what works and what doesn't, he has turned the five Growing Power greenhouses into an experimental lab. They represent a closed system, in which everything produced goes back into producing something more. At one end of Greenhouse 2, twelve rabbits in cages wiggle their flop ears. Their pellets, along with the shredded newspaper in their cages, will go to the worms. Not far from the boxes of worms, volunteers tend an experiment in food production. It combines two techniques: aquaculture, or fish farming in containers, and hydroponics, growing plants in water rather than soil. The manure and exhaled ammonia from the tilapia are fed into the hydroponics trays. The hydroponic onions are doing well. The sixty-day watercress is being harvested in thirty days.

These techniques are not new; hydroponics, for instance, are thought to have fed the gardens of Babylon.

But the idea is to look for new applications, new forms of intensive farming that use as little energy, labor, and natural resources as possible—applications that, like the Market Basket program, can be adapted anywhere in the world. If a community has a four-hundred-gallon tank for tilapia rather than a two-hundred-gallon one, no problem. Use what you have. Make it work. The resulting benefits include fresh, locally distributed produce, but they also may encompass a stronger tax base, city beautification, and an income that could make farming pay.

"In the conventional system," Will says, "the farmer is generally the loser, getting ten percent on the dollar. We want to create a scenario where everybody wins."

Will's work has captured the attention of representatives from global organizations. The Heifer Project, an international nonprofit that donates livestock to families around the world, underwrites Growing Power, as does the Jane B. Pettit Foundation; the Wisconsin Department of Agriculture, Trade, and Consumer Protection; and the USDA, among other organizations. Members of the Heifer Project have attended Will's workshops. People in Angola want Will's volunteers to come and train them.

They recognize that the work being done in Growing Power's greenhouses could address several problems of the world: Food shortages. Overuse of chemicals. Untillable soil. Limited growing seasons. Even the problem of fish waste, which I didn't even *know* was a problem. Apparently large-scale fish waste plagues a good share of the world. Add that waste to compost and feed it to the worms, and voilà: instant soil.

The experiments going on in Will's greenhouses, just like other greenhouses around the world, might mean that people in Mexico and Africa could all produce the food they need, right where they live. Alone, this won't answer the question of how we'll feed a world population of eight billion people by the year 2025; that's where the debate over high-yield farming and transgenic seed kicks in. But the small and intensive farm practices could be adopted with no political powers to circumvent, no cultural lines to cross. This is when you start to see how these five little greenhouses in urban Milwaukee could make a difference.

People fear failure, but as Will says, nothing's ever going to be perfect right at the beginning. You just take it one step at a time. For example, he says, "The fish machine is a culmination of all the mistakes I've made before. I tell people the first rule of farming is, 'Don't panic.'"

∞

Will doesn't want to sit around in committee meetings talking policy and how great it would be to feed the world. He just wants to get on with it. He wants earthworms gobbling up thousands of pounds of garbage and doing the alchemy of castings, and eager little shoots of watercress poking up from narrow trays fed by fish water. Wanting everyone to have decent food is about as nonviolent and non-obtrusive a wish as you could get, yet it is one of the most provocative issues in the world.

For Will, no matter how you globalize it, the need comes back to fundamental issues, like kids in his own neighborhood struggling to make it through the day without having their basic needs met. "You don't have to have much money to be happy," Will says. "But you've got to have food."

The world needs people who can look at a chicken

19

tractor or a rabbit and visualize the end of starvation. The world also needs people who can teach the rest of us to do the same thing. While Will raises some of the biggest and most daunting questions of our global citizenship, he answers them in his own way: Do what you can in your own backyard. If we all did that, the world would take care of itself.

Will isn't out to change the ways of multinational food producers or foreign governments. But he is spurring people to turn the weedy lot on the corner into a field of cucumbers and kale, and he's probably inspiring a few others to turn off the TV and make dinner for the family. Think globally; act locally. And pose some thought-provoking questions along the way.

wild one

Never does nature say one thing and wisdom another.
—Juvenal

Before the lawnmower, before chemical fertilizers, before rakes and mulchers and composters and trimmers, plants grew up and plants died down, trees shed their leaves and fed the soil, and seeds found their way to fertile ground and settled in and put down roots—or they didn't—and it was fine either way. This system worked well for millions of years, and then the Perfect Yard was introduced.

The Perfect Yard had only one kind of grass—all one length, with no sign of weeds. It had flowers, lots of them, including bulbs shipped in from all parts of the world. It had some flowers that needed acidic soil and some that needed alkaline, some that needed a lot of water and some that withstood heat and drought. Creating the Perfect Yard could be satisfying, but it also cost a lot of money, a lot of water, a lot of energy in the form of jealousy and inadequacy if your neighbor did it better and exhaustion if you did it better, and in some cases, a lot of changes to the environment. We're still not sure what it may cost in the end.

Virginia Umberger is not a Perfect Yard kind of person. In fact, she's what some would call a rebel, which is a bit amusing, considering that she's ninety-two years old and looks like a school crossing guard. But she is trying to get *rid* of the bulbs in her yard; planting them years ago constitutes one of her greatest lifetime regrets. She is eliminating as much grass from her property as possible. And she lets the enormous oak trees in her Chicago-suburb yard have their way. They dictate the amount of sunlight her flowers receive, provide all the mulch, and determine where and how far the plants will grow. It's only fair. Even though Virginia has lived on this property for more than fifty years, the trees were here first.

❧

Virginia stands about five feet tall, wears a sweatshirt, khaki pants, and glasses that might seem big for her face but are balanced by a cloud of white hair. "Would you like to see the garden?" she asks. It's about two in the afternoon, and the sun has passed its noon peak and has started sending its slanted light back toward the east. This means that the woodland garden surrounding her house, a carpet of plants sheltered by the oak trees, is sparkling just a bit, as though little crystals have planted themselves everywhere.

Virginia immediately demonstrates why she's a natural teacher: She knows everything. As she walks from plant to plant, she points out individual species, calls them by their botanical names, and gives a bit of history about them in the most unassuming and personal way. There's the *Jeffersonia diphylla*, better known as twinleaf, which, while pretty enough, is a stingy nod to Thomas

Jefferson; it's the only plant named for him, despite the monumental contributions he made to botany. Under an oak tree is an entire blanket of *Podophyllum peltatum*, which the rest of us would call mayapple, looking like little umbrellas hugging the ground. And then there's *Hamamelis*, or witch hazel. "I introduced it because it belonged here," Virginia says.

Virginia may have inherited both her knowledge and her modesty from her father, an orchardist and plantsman who took her for walks in the woods when she was growing up in Indiana. At an early age, she learned to recognize native woodland plants, such as hepatica and wild trillium with its three-petaled white flowers. Soon she was rattling off Latin names for the woodland plants she crouched over and studied.

When Virginia and her husband moved to this property, she took classes at the Morton Arboretum in Lisle, Illinois, studying with May Theilgaard Watts, a naturalist, poet, and artist who wrote several books, including the groundbreaking *Reading the Landscape of America*. The book was first published in 1957 but has recently been rereleased. In it, Watts plays a naturalist Sherlock Holmes, visiting everything from the pygmy forest on the Pacific coast to a northern Wisconsin campsite and, through careful observation and an encyclopedic collection of facts, determines the plants that have been part of the area's history and the ecology that made the place what it is.

In one chapter, for instance, she describes and illustrates how cows "prune" hawthorn tree seedlings. When the seedlings are very young and their thorns still tender, the cows graze the plants into a cone shape. When the cone reaches a certain height, the cows can't reach its top growth, which continues unabated, turning the cone into an hourglass shape. And when the top growth spreads out, it shades the cone below it, which dies off. This leaves the horizontal spreading branches for which pasture hawthorns are known. Without the ecological interaction with the cows, the tree would grow differently.

These kinds of ideas from the book and its author set Virginia on a new course, exploring ways to garden without disturbing nature's manifest destiny. She became something of a garden shepherd, nudging the flowers one direction or another, and setting a few boundaries by edging beds with small tree branches, but her rule is the way of ecology: mess with it as little as possible. Nature knows what it's doing. Eventually, she joined the Wild Ones, an anti-lawn group that spurns expanses of grass and believes in native plants. For years now, Virginia has been living and informally teaching what Watts taught her.

"Look at that," she says, leaning over a pile of leaves. She has spotted an *Iris cristata*, a tiny purple flower barely peeking through the mulch. She clears the leaves around it to give it room to grow. "It's native but not indigenous," she says matter-of-factly, meaning that it's native to the United States but not to this area of the country. I'm stunned that she knew it was *there*.

We're heading around to the front of the house. Almost completely shaded by the canopy of the oaks, there's a secret-garden feeling to the beds, which encircle her house, right up to the understory trees that buffer her from the road in front.

She points out an eighteen-inch tulip tree that seeded itself in the yard. "This is not tulip tree territory," Virginia says. "But I've decided to leave it here. It thrills me that it picked its spot. I'm not sure the spot is a good one, but mentally, I can't make myself move it." Other plants are welcome just where they landed. The bloodroot, wood-land phlox, goldenseal, and violets can all stay and spread to their heart's content. In fact, Virginia finds great plea-sure in noting how nature plants its own garden. Squir-rels gave her buckeyes, and the Dutchman's-breeches and anemones planted themselves by the driveway, creating what Virginia says is "the prettiest mix possible."

Across the road from Virginia's house is another garden, this one in full sun. It started out as a vegetable garden in the early 1950s, but for years Virginia has given it over to natural plantings of sun-loving natives, with just a bit of space devoted to raspberries, currants, tomatoes, beets, cucumbers, and herbs.

A lot of the woodland plants have found their way over to this sunny spot, Virginia says. "The Dutchman's-breeches have come over, and the bloodroot. A lot of things you can't explain," she says. *Dicentra eximia*, or fringed bleeding heart, has seeded itself around the garden, "and I couldn't be happier," Virginia says.

There are more lessons here: The shade garden around the house requires little maintenance because the soil is stable, but this sun garden requires constant work since the soil is always disturbed. You can do away with ants by mixing about a quarter teaspoon boric acid with a tablespoon honey and setting it around the garden. And the secret of good soil is to mix one part soil, one part compost, one part pea gravel, and one part sand.

About the time we're admiring the celadon color of a

maple's leaves against the brilliant blue sky, two visitors arrive. Janet and Sharon have just been to a garden club meeting, one that Virginia skipped, she tells me later, because today's presentation was on flower wholesaling. She is too polite to say any more than this, but from the look on her face, it's easy to see that she considers the business of wholesaling flowers as unnatural as those bulbs that threatened to take over her garden.

The two women give Virginia a hug and comment on how beautiful everything looks. It's clear that Virginia is the elder stateswoman of the garden club, like the teacher everybody loved and still comes back to visit.

Virginia and Janet wander off, but Sharon stays nearby and studies the garden. This is what people do in Virginia's gardens. They study, they admire, they absorb.

"We used to live in this neighborhood," Sharon says. "My kids knew Virginia as 'the gourd lady.' She'd turn gourds into piggy banks and rabbits."

Now Virginia's impact has more to do with her knowledge of mayapples and Virginia bluebells. "My kids have learned from her, and I have two grandchildren who have gardened with her," Sharon says. She tells me she has a redbud tree that was transplanted from this sunny space. "When it's blooming," she says, "that's Virginia in my yard."

❧

"Gourds are *in*," Virginia says, leaning over her kitchen table and opening a book of gourd crafts. She is flipping through pages with full-color how-to photographs, showing close-ups of hands carving, staining, and wood-burning gourds.

She has just introduced me to her collection of gourds, starting with a few small wood-burned ones hanging on her bathroom wall. Outdoors, she's the Wild One. But when she comes inside, she's all gourds.

On the dining room table is a centerpiece Virginia made. Its grapevine base is anchored in a tuna can, and the gourds arranged on it have been sprayed with a satin finish. "My husband and I used to go places and see lamp bases or swags," Virginia says, "and I'd think, how could you do that with gourds?"

There are Santas made out of gourds, a tiny Nativity scene set into a hollowed-out gourd, and an owl shaped from gourds and loofah sponges, which, I didn't know, are members of the gourd family. Like trillium or hepatica, gourds are native plants. The yellow-flowered gourd, for instance, is native to the eastern United States and northern Mexico, but it's been cultivated for so many centuries that it's no longer found in the wild.

Virginia turns the key in the lock of her sunporch. A shrine of sorts, this room measures about eight by ten feet, creating eighty square feet of display space. In it are a table and chairs, and nothing else but gourds. Strung up on a chain made out of cane all the way around the perimeter of the room and just two inches below the ceiling hang dozens of gourds of all colors and descriptions. Some are pear shaped, some round. Virginia leads me all around the room, showing me each of the gourds on the shelves and tables.

Gourds are classified as a hard-shelled ornamental fruit that, as Virginia readily knows, belong to the *Cucurbitaceae* family. Cucumbers and pumpkins are gourds; so are watermelons and squash. But the ones in Virginia's sunroom were not grown for food. Instead, they're white-flowered gourds, a species cultivated for use as musical instruments and containers. Having collected gourds from all over the world, Virginia points out a few African specimens in her collection. Typically, she tells me, they're used to carry milk, oil, or blood. One has a long neck that's twisted and tied in knots. This knotting is a delicate procedure, Virginia tells me. "You have to do it at just the right time."

A jug from New Zealand sits on the floor. Intricately carved, its design bears the stamp of the man who decorated it. He had quite a colorful life, Virginia says. He danced in the courts of Indonesia and lived in a cave for a while. She corresponded with him for years. "I never thought any information I could provide would be as important as what he knew," she says. When he died, the National Museum of Art in New Zealand collected his paintings and carved gourds, and they contacted Virginia, who sent them all the letters he'd ever written her.

This is the binding tie of gourds, which stretches beyond a fascination with gardening and laces together related interests in history, art, and culture. Virginia tells me gourds provide a sense of connection with the pioneers who used them and with even earlier peoples, since remnants of gourds have been found in ancient caves.

Virginia and her husband became *the* gourd couple in the area. He remembered gourds from his childhood, when his family used them as dippers for well water or containers for food. Once the Umbergers started growing them, they looked for gourds in their travels. The couple brought home gourds of all descriptions, many of them now displayed in that musty sunporch. One, a six-foot-long gourd shaped like an out-of-control French loaf, was transported in their car halfway across the country. "We got a lot of looks," she says. Virginia and her husband gave presentations to school kids. They made wreaths and swags in a building adjacent to their house (still labeled with a sign that reads CURING SHED), where they also offered classes in making grapevine baskets and curing gourds. It's easy to detect that they had fun together. But that was a long time ago now. Her husband died in 1978.

Even though the heyday of her gourd life happened thirty years ago, Virginia has none of the sadness or regret of a fading movie star. She is Greta Garbo as she might have been if she hadn't been so darn reclusive. Outside, she walks her gardens like a long-legged and graceful bird, and inside she hovers a moment to point out a gourd with a particularly comely shape or an example of the most intricate hand-carving on a gourd depicting Peruvian farmers.

Gourds are "products of nature and each one is unique," Virginia says. "No two in the world are alike." *They're like snowflakes*, I think, looking at an especially rotund gourd. Thankfully, they don't fall from the sky.

⌘

We're in her basement, which is something of a gourd museum. This is where she does her limited gourd crafts today. Gourds are everywhere, in troughlike wooden bowls, on shelves, and in baskets. One large basket holds a selection in the softest shades of orange, brown, green, and rust. Nearby is an old metal desk with a GOURDS MUST PREDOMINATE bumper sticker on one drawer. Inside the file drawer is a folder of information, including tearsheets from *National Geographic* magazines of the last century, all showing native people working with gourds. Virginia and her husband used this information for the programs they presented to school groups and garden clubs.

Those programs might have included fun gourd facts, like the fact that some gourd vines grow to be fifty feet long. Or, because gourds have unisexual flowers and the pollen is heavy and sticky, the plants rely on insects, especially honeybees, for pollination. The bees' free-for-all means that buying gourd seeds is an iffy proposition; sometimes the resulting plants match the picture on the package, sometimes they don't. "You never know what you're going to get," Virginia says. My favorite gourd fact involves the *Cucumis humifructus* gourd in southern Africa. It bears underground fruits, which are dug up and eaten by aardvarks. Aardvarks dig holes for their dung, then cover the holes with loose soil. As a result, any seeds that pass through the animals are planted directly into a perfectly prepared and fertilized garden.

30

On a board at the bottom of the stairs, propped up along the wall, are pinned samples of different natural materials, accompanied by labels. LIPSTICK POD: HAWAII, one reads. SEA GRAPE, reads another.

"I sent away to a firm that offers exotics so I could use them in wreaths," Virginia says. She chose them for their form, texture, and color, spurning manufactured trims that would have added, she says, a "jarring note."

The basement smells like a mixture of wet concrete blocks, remnants of an old coal chute, and damp laundry hung on the line. It's a natural kind of smell, like the smell of spring dirt, and it's comforting, if a little moist. In the "doing room," there's a washer and dryer, a stove that Virginia once used for canning, and a utility sink. Several gourds are soaking in a pail of water, the first step before they're skinned with steel wool and a stiff brush to later be made into a wreath. She stops to check on them, opening the pail. A smell worse than old watermelon rinds and rotting potatoes in the middle of July fills the room. "My smelling is bad," she says, "but even I know this stinks."

She gives me the tour of it all with the greatest dignity. One back room is lined with citrus and onion sacks made of netting that hang from nails in the wall. Each sack holds a different shape of gourd: spoon, egg, round, pendant, bell, and others, just a sample of the seven hundred species in the gourd order. At one time, the crafts that Virginia and her husband made probably consumed this many gourds in a matter of weeks. Now the demand has slowed, but she still uses them in occasional wreaths. The past two years, she's made five-foot-diameter wreaths at Christmastime for her church's silent auction. They sold for no less than five hundred dollars apiece.

⸙

So much of Virginia's life has passed. You can feel it when you're in her basement with the dried flowers in plastic bags hanging upside down from a bamboo screen, her daughter's now-yellowed school project from probably fifty years ago, and a dusty Christmas swag of gourds mounted on a piece of board with chicken wire. The crown-shaped gourd at the top is broken, "but it's okay to have imperfection," Virginia says. And it is. It's also okay to have a past. The fact is, that basement with its aging treasures is not where Virginia lives. She lives in the present, among the Jacob's ladder and the rue anemone out in the sun-dappled beds.

Clearly, her love for the natural garden has grown stronger in the many decades since she walked alongside her father in the woods of Indiana. She's pleased to see that more people are coming to appreciate the value of woodlands and natural gardens. "Wildflowers have their association with animals and insects in the environment," she says. "So for the health of the environment, we should use natives for interchange."

If there's any question about what that means, think of aardvarks and their relationship to underground gourds. *That's* natural interchange.

She doesn't say this the way a teacher would say it, though. She simply states it as a possible idea and her own personal opinion. In fact, she defers to Barbara Kingsolver's *Prodigal Summer*, a book given to her by a friend. "The author speaks of the importance of native trees," she says. "If a tree is cut down, the birds and insects are gone. That made an impact on me. It's true of little plants and big ones." I'm guessing that Virginia knew this before most of us were born.

Sharon, the garden club friend who visited Virginia in the sun garden, says that it's an enormous gift to the community to have someone so knowledgeable around. Virginia keeps records of her plants and their activity. "She's impacted every one of us with the tours of her garden, her knowledge, and humility," she says. Maybe most telling of all, students from Morton Arboretum, where Virginia first studied with May Theilgaard Watts, now visit Virginia's garden to observe and study, maybe to become a Wild One someday.

It's nearing six P.M., and the late afternoon light now makes the entire yard glimmer. At more than twice my age, Virginia is still as energetic as when I arrived. I get the feeling that she could whip off the botanical names of the first half of the plants in a Horticulture A to Z manual, and I'd be lucky to remember that *M* comes after *L*.

Virginia is a woman in the moment, taking time with whoever visits her garden. Her husband has been gone for almost a quarter of a century. Her daughter lives in another part of the world. Yet her world is still as current and alive as it was when she was sharing gourd information with the artist in New Zealand. She'll be going to bed about nine o'clock, she says, which is her regular bedtime, because tomorrow is a big, although typical, day. She'll be visiting gardens with friends, taking part in a community celebration of gardens by the river, and hosting whoever happens to stop by in between. She's gone through a whole life of learning, and she keeps moving forward rather than looking back.

And the one thing she would tell people about gardening?

"Love it," she says, "Love working in the soil and the anticipation of growth. Love the whole cycle."

Out by the car, I take one last look at the woodland garden, sparkling in the late-afternoon sun. On the hood of my car, right by the windshield, is a small branch deposited from the oak tree overhead. At home, I would have picked it off and tossed it over by a bush somewhere. But this place makes me feel a bit more reverent. So in this sanctuary of oak trees and woodland plants, I pick up the branch, look around, and lay it carefully in a bed next to the foundation of the house. Virginia will take care of it, I figure, just like the earth itself.

interplanting

The earth is my mother—and on her bosom I will recline.
—Tecumseh

hen Priscilla Logan stands outside her straw-bale cabin in the mountains near Santa Fe, New Mexico, she is amidst ponderosa pines and large rock outcrops. Rock barriers known as check dams lie in between the pines and rolls of the land, forming gentle curves. Many of them were built to control erosion by the Work Progress Administration in the 1930s. Others have been here since the 1800s, when early settlers grazed their flocks of goats and sheep.

This is a place that belongs to bear and elk, to people who step lightly upon the land, and to those who look toward the earth for guidance. Priscilla, having come to these mountains from Iowa by way of Arizona and Colorado, appreciates what nature has to teach us if we'll only pay attention. The "three sisters," she says, are a good example.

The three sisters of corn, beans, and squash originally were grown in all the Americas by native people who planted them together in a functional interrelationship. The corn stalks grew tall and strong, which gave the beans a place to climb. The beans provided nitrogen for the corn. In turn, the squash plants spread out at the base of the corn and beans, conserving moisture and shading the ground from weeds so that all three plants could draw the nutrients they needed from the soil.

The interconnectedness of the three is "a beautiful thing," says Priscilla. A teacher, retired from the school system in Santa Fe, she says that the three sisters are a metaphor for living in the Southwest. "How do we help each other, conserve water, and provide nutrients for each other?"

These are questions she's been concerned with for the past forty-one years, ever since she and her dad traveled from her home state of Iowa to Colorado, joined a team of twenty-five riders on horseback for a four-week wilderness trip, and along the way met a man from Santa Fe. The next summer, she worked at a Santa Fe guest ranch and fell in love with the Southwest. That was 1961; she moved to New Mexico in 1976. And in 1992, she initiated a project that has a lot to teach all of us about the value of kids, water, gardens, and protecting the earth.

⚬

At the time, Priscilla was working at Santa Fe's Sweeney Elementary School, where the student population is 94 percent low income; traditionally, only 30 percent stayed in school from kindergarten to fifth grade. Having worked as a reading specialist, Priscilla found herself suddenly in charge of one hundred fourth, fifth, and sixth graders, all with special needs of one kind or another.

Sweeney is a one-story, sun-bleached building set in a bleak neighborhood of juniper and piñon trees and trailers, across the street from a four-story building of low-income housing. The school's kids and parents had never had a community issue to rally around before, until Priscilla and the students made two observations: Fish had disappeared from the Santa Fe River below the sewage treatment plant, and levels of nitrates were showing up in wells in the river-basin area.

Priscilla has a background in sustainable agriculture and water retainment, so she pays attention to these things. But she encouraged the kids to pay attention, too. Here were investigative problems that, to be corrected, demanded a knowledge of math, science, and language. Each month, Priscilla took students to the Santa Fe River to record the chlorine levels, and she set up a program at the school to analyze wells in their neighborhood.

"I decided that the best way people learn is to get them interested in topics and have their work make a difference," Priscilla says.

Through their research, the students discovered that wetlands, which retain water during periods of high runoff, also clean polluted water. This, they postulated, could be a solution for the Santa Fe River. Priscilla and the students decided to build a model storm water purification system to show government officials, in the hopes that the officials would build a wetlands for the river. They would build their model at the school, creating a purification system to clean hydrocarbons out of the rainwater running off from the teacher's parking lot and the roof.

The students graphed the water runoff, determined where the model wetlands needed to be, and started digging the system. Despite their enthusiasm, the project was too big for their shovels and spades. In fact, they calculated that digging the system by hand would take two-and-a-half years. It was time to enlist community support.

Parents took part in the project in a number of ways, from driving backhoes to providing moral support. The students, Priscilla told them, could work outside as long as one or both of their parents were there. And if the parents couldn't come, they were welcome to send food for the others.

The parents not only sent feasts of food, but they helped in other ways, offering any time or money they could afford. All of it counted, Priscilla says, remembering the day she received an envelope with a one-dollar bill inside. A note read, *"Para tu proyecto,"* or "For your project."

The effort resembled a tangle of corn, beans, and squash, all growing there together, all helping each other, shading out any problems, standing strong and tall, and providing nutrients for one another. One day, Priscilla says, they needed to move six tons of river rock from one spot to another, and she had no idea how they'd get it done. The kids adopted a "no problem" attitude. They brought out buckets and formed brigades, and in twenty-minute shifts throughout the day, they moved it all, one rock at a time.

Photos from the time show the expected mess of construction. Piles of rock and desert soil were stacked along deep trenches. In the future pond, the liner looked like a huge black tarp stretched out in a cavernous hole. But by the time the project was done, the kids and their parents, with the support of local businesses, had built a three-stage system complete with a sedimentation basin, eight-ton rock filter, constructed wetlands, pond, and overflow ditches. Then, as the crowning touch, they ran an irrigation ditch off the overflow and set up drip irrigation to water the new habitat garden—about 150 native trees, shrubs, and plants, including willows now fifteen feet high that have created a thicket habitat for warblers and finches.

"That kind of empowerment doesn't come just with a piece of paper and a pencil," Priscilla says. "It really comes from doing something that involves your heart."

At the conclusion of the project, every student—including those who had started the year with poor English or language skills—wrote, illustrated, and hand-bound a book. At the end of the year, Priscilla held a symposium for about twenty city, county, state, and federal officials. They listened to the kids read their books, toured the wetlands area, and heard the students' conclusions that the Santa Fe River needed a wetlands. "They were astounded," Priscilla says. "That just made those kids feel more special."

Despite the impression the students made, the officials inferred that a wetlands wasn't possible. Two years later, Priscilla found an individual who donated eight riverside acres to a children's non-profit. She helped create a wetlands there, where hundreds of Santa Fe students continue to study river restoration. There are now fish in the river, and the sewage treatment plant no longer uses chlorine. "I like to think," Priscilla says, "it's all because some kids cared."

There hasn't been a project like it before or since, but the impact of the wetlands and garden project isn't lost. The kids from that year are now grown up, and every once in a while some will come back and check on the wetlands. Some, Priscilla knows, are in college studying environmental issues.

Priscilla has been retired for four years, but she still is passionate about conservation, kids, and education, and she lives a life wedded to her convictions. When the worries of a limited water supply and a growing Santa Fe population weigh heavily on her, she retreats to the mountains for a week or two, where she can think about the interrelationship of people and plants in the quiet of the cabin she and her friend Michael built.

Located about an hour-and-a-half outside Santa Fe, it's set up in the mountains, the ones that turn strawberry pink and red in the setting sun. Like centuries-old dwellings in Hungary and the Czech Republic, the cabin is made of straw bales set on a raised foundation, supported by wood beams, held together by intricate interweavings of rebar and chicken wire, and covered on the interior and exterior with layers of cement. The straw insulates the five-hundred-square-foot cabin. Priscilla doesn't know the precise number of bales used in the cabin, although it was a large truckload. But she can tell you just how far the foundation sits off the ground on its stilts at one corner of the house and how far it sits on another corner, allowing for the slope of the mountain and large insulated basement.

The straw-bale cabin is located on twenty acres of land in a spot that lay unpopulated for two hundred years. Priscilla and Michael bought the land in 1994, drawn by the two ponds, the seventy-foot ponderosas, and the curving dams on the valley floor. Near the cabin stands a greenhouse with a three-foot-tall, five hundred-gallon horse tank filled with water. With the help of an aluminum stove, the water can be heated and used as a hot tub or as a heat sink for the greenhouse. In the winter, Priscilla grows chard, kale, parsley, and herbs that don't mind being frozen.

She also has a fruit/nut orchard and vegetable gardens,

composting toilets, and a worm farm in the basement. She plants habitat for birds—feeders are out because of the bears. She grows penstemons and sunflowers, both for the birds and as a fire retardant. Catnip keeps the squash bugs and Colorado potato beetle population down.

Despite all this, she doesn't claim to be self-sufficient. She's taken enough classes to know there's a difference between treading lightly and living off the land. Still, she works in concert with nature wherever possible, continuing to learn and, even though she's retired, to become a better teacher.

"My gardens look like a jungle," she says. "Plants grow where they want to grow." She turns the soil "because we have such a dry climate that I want to hold the water down deep." As a result, seeds that come off her dill and fennel and carrots are worked into the soil and come up where they want. "It's a very productive jungle," she says.

∽

I've just been watching a ten-minute videotape that Priscilla produced about using the outdoors as a classroom. The narrator has a Hispanic accent and soft voice, the music is light and friendly, and the video shows dozens of kids—girls with ponytails and braids, boys with buzz cuts and blue sweatshirts—digging in the dirt, carrying buckets of water, and walking around their Santa Fe school in the New Mexico sun with clipboards and rakes. Every once in a while I stop the tape to rewind, and the TV reverts to a sitcom with raucous characters and ill-timed laughter. The change is startling and unwelcome. It's a reminder of how healing nature can be for kids who are bombarded by the laugh track of life.

In outdoor classrooms, at least 90 percent of learning is hands-on. Kids who learn by doing retain 75 percent of the information they're taught, Priscilla says. When students teach each other, the retention rate rises to 90 percent. This, among other reasons, is why Priscilla has developed a three-year program in which she trains teachers to set up outdoor classrooms at their own schools. Since 1998, it has been adopted by schools in three school districts.

During the first year, Priscilla's main goal is to help teachers envision a classroom without walls, desks, or chairs. Teachers take kids outside for class activities, and they invite volunteer mentors to help work with the kids. Activities in the outdoor classroom are aligned with state math and science standards, and then evaluated through surveys completed by teachers, mentors, and students. In the first year that Priscilla did the training, a ten-inch stack of surveys was fed to a Texas university computer for analysis. The results substantiated what Priscilla already knew: In the outdoor classroom, students not only learn math and science, they learn critical thinking skills, teamwork, and language skills, too.

The second year, Priscilla trains the teachers to do a school site analysis, looking at both environmental and human resources. This is not a cursory examination. Outdoors, assignments inspire students to think like detectives. At one school, a teacher in a polar fleece sweatshirt printed with Native American petroglyphs gives her elementary school kids clipboards and a set of instructions, and they leave the four walls of the classroom and step into the bright sun and chilly weather of the Santa Fe day. To find out where rainwater goes in their schoolyard, they look at the roof to see where water is channeled as it falls. They look at piles of leaves to see if they were gathered by wind or water. They look at runoff around their school grounds. And they mark their findings on a school site map.

They do the same with questions of erosion. Where do they see signs of it? Is it caused by rain or wind? Where does water move the dry desert soil, and where does it collect? The students imbed thermometers into the hard ground and compare the temperatures. Where does the sun warm the soil the most? Would this be a good place for a garden?

In the third year, the teachers write a grant proposal or ask the support of the community to build their dream outdoor classroom. This is where the research comes in, as does plenty of imagination. In the outdoor classroom at one elementary school, children sit on big boulders along a path outside their school library. In this literary garden, plants are tied to favorite children's books. Under a peach tree, for instance, a sign for the book *James and the Giant Peach* invites kids to sit and read. The garden, with boulders donated by a child's grandfather, will soon have more comfortable benches. So when teachers and the librarian want to read to a class, they can bring the children into this garden, where the kids can immerse themselves in sensory stimulation along with the words of *Charlotte's Web* or *The Grouchy Ladybug*.

Other schools have done equally imaginative projects. One is planning a botanical garden for its new high school campus, where students will plant native species, including medicinal herbs, grasses, and cactus. Teachers anticipate that the students will create and publish a student-friendly plant classification key and give tours to people in the community. Another school is building its own scale replica of the solar system, using a bowling ball for the sun, a walnut for Jupiter, and a pinhead for Pluto. The system extends from the schoolyard to a business across the street, where the first star will be located.

"Every school has come up with what they want," Priscilla says.

Projects like the wetlands and related gardens teach kids to use higher-level thinking skills, as well as the competencies measured on standardized tests, she says. "That's the kind of learning we want to get going." Give kids something meaningful to do, she adds, and they'll learn. They'll learn math, science, and language, and probably much more.

~～

Priscilla's work is rooted in the research and analysis of education, but she's also interested in ideas beyond anything we can currently measure. About ten years ago, a presentation about labyrinths caught her attention. "I try to listen when my mind tells me this is something I need to hear," she says. She realized that she needed a labyrinth, although she didn't know why, so she talked to a labyrinth designer and learned that dowsing was the key. "The earth tells you where to put the labyrinth," Priscilla explains. Dowsing is better known as the process of searching for water with the help of a divining rod. But it can be used to determine sites for labyrinths, too. This, Priscilla knows, sounds a little out of the mainstream, but she doesn't question that it works.

Priscilla built her first labyrinth near her straw-bale cabin. Intrigued by the history of labyrinths—the designs appear on everything from Celtic rocks to Crete coins and Native American pottery—she values the design even though, like the rest of the world, no one knows for sure what they're for or why they have such a calming effect. "There are so many right and left turns," she says, "some people say it helps balance different sides of the brain." Now she installs labyrinths at schools and at facilities for people with special needs.

"I'm always humbled," she says, because repeatedly she thinks the labyrinth belongs one place, and the earth tells her something else. When she designed one for Sweeney Elementary School, the dowsing led her to an area near the school bus loading area, bordered on two sides by cement. The dowsing determined where the center of the labyrinth should be and the size of the seven rings in this particular labyrinth design. Unsure that the labyrinth would fit in the space she'd been told, she and the kids nevertheless set out on faith, laying out the rocks they'd chosen to form the labyrinth's continuous circular path.

Not only did it fit, but it was perfectly centered. "We ended up with less than five inches of extra space on either side," she says.

The kids' reactions to walking the labyrinth vary from getting dizzy to saying, "When can we do it again?" But unanimously, Priscilla says, "people come out and breathe more deeply and say 'that was wonderful.'"

A labyrinth at a local middle school will soon be constructed, but the school has a unique idea: every student will pick out a rock and paint it. Then, with Priscilla's help, they'll build the labyrinth with their own "pet" rocks. Like gardens, Priscilla says, labyrinths offer kids something they don't get enough of these days. "With kids, eighty percent of their time is in malls or on streets or playgrounds or in houses. They're not even touching the earth with their feet. How can we expect kids or adults to have a relationship with the earth if they don't spend time with it?"

∽

Of all the projects Priscilla has done, building the model wetlands at Sweeney Elementary was the most impossible. "If I had it to do over again, I wouldn't have done it," she says. "It was absolutely insane." But she admits that it was a miracle, too. With up to one hundred kids working outside, she says, "never did I have an injury. Never did I have a discipline problem. I had doubts whether we could do it, but the kids were just unquenchable. They knew what they wanted and they moved ahead."

As a result, quiet kids in Minnie Mouse T-shirts stood up and gave presentations. Little boys explained to their elders how to stop erosion. Kids made holes in the hard desert earth by pounding a length of rebar with a rock to plant a willow cutting. And they all worked together with the earth, like the three sisters, intertwining their roots and protecting one another.

Like all educators, Priscilla faces financial cuts that make it more difficult for schools to find funds for teacher training. It will be more important, she says, for outside sources and people in the community to get involved, to see the value of gardens and solar systems as outdoor classrooms and help teachers create them.

"Beautiful things are everywhere," Priscilla says. "Kids know that, and that's what keeps me going."

gardens that nourish

At Yellowstone National Park, a display about buffalo includes an interesting piece of garden trivia. Actually, it's not trivial at all, as it has to do with the ecosystem and the interconnectedness of all things. The display explains that buffalo helped create conditions to host plants growing on the plains. This process started whenever a buffalo wallowed in the dirt both to cool itself and to discourage insects, which were less interested in dusty buffalo. Other buffalo would wallow in the same spot, and pretty soon the wallowing hole would expand. When it rained, the hole filled with water, and even though the water evaporated, the soil around the hole became a moist host for seeds. When seeds blew or were dropped in, they sprung up in the wallow, initiating another microgarden. Granted, the buffalo might stampede it later, but it was there just the same.

This started me thinking about the many ways that we all create and nourish the right conditions for growth.

It makes me think of a friend who has worked as a federal prosecutor in South Dakota. She saw the worst of what American society and the poverty of Native American reservations dish up—abuse of all kinds, murder, rape. Many of the people she prosecuted look like your next-door neighbor, except that they had a little problem with a knife slipping, she says, or just a touch of anger control when they held a can of gasoline in one hand and a match in the other. She said it got to the point after a while that she walked down the street and looked at complete strangers and wondered, "What are *you* capable of?"

This is why she often thought about a woman she worked with in the past, a woman who, spring through fall, did the simplest thing almost every Monday morning: She brought flowers from her garden to work. Sometimes it would be a single rose or iris or a bunch of daisies. She set the vase on her desk, and every time my friend walked by, she was reminded that there's a world outside the courtroom.

She'd ask the gardener, "What did you do this weekend?" and the gardener would say, "Well, I had a wonderful couple of days. I spent them on my knees."

My friend would study the contents of the vase, notice the delicacy of the petals, the perfection of the leaves. "It made me realize that there's something so much bigger than we are," she says. "Those flowers balanced and replenished us."

It's interesting to think of all the ways gardens feed us. They give us carrots and potatoes and, in good years, meaty tomatoes with no spots. They give us flowers that are a banquet for the eyes. And they satisfy a hunger for peace and calm and *okayness* in the world. I think that's what truly feeds us because all of our actions, including what we plant and what we harvest and eat, stem from those thoughts and ideas. So the real nourishment we need is to have a belief system that satisfies us and helps us grow, that gives us the building blocks of a happy and fulfilled life.

Don and Bev Sudbury fortify the lives of others through multitask gardening in Salt Lake City, Utah. The gardening résumé of this retired couple would fill this entire book. They're both Master Gardeners for one simple reason: When Don took the course, Bev thought it looked interesting, so she did too.

Well, one thing led to another, and pretty soon they were planting gardens in their back yard. Maybe a few daylilies. What the heck, how about several hundred? They expanded their flower beds around the side of their small house, then out around to the front. Don decorated the garden by making a gong out of a manhole cover and hoisting an old bent-out-of-shape sousaphone into the lower branches of a tree. Then he learned all the botanical names of all the plants, becoming known as enough of an expert on them that he was asked to present a lecture to the local Master Gardeners. The Sudburys designed and planted a children's garden at the University of Utah's Botanical Garden and Arboretum. They are helping to restore a little-known and long-neglected private sculpture garden in Salt Lake City. And in their free time, they stay at home and water their flowers. Sometimes they'll be part of a garden tour, and about seven hundred people drop by.

But Don and Bev have made some great friends this way. One of their favorite families happened to stop in years ago on their way through town. They were total strangers, but Don and Bev gave them a tour, concluding with their hundreds of *Hemerocallis*. Even though the families live in different states, they have been in touch ever since.

That kind of connection just comes naturally in a garden. Take, for example, the many efforts across the country to give at-risk adults new opportunities through gardening. One such program operated in Washington,

D.C., for several years. Tended by homeless people, this organic garden at the junction of New Jersey and Massachusetts avenues sat just a few blocks north of the U.S. Capitol. It was started by an executive who felt that the plight of the homeless was too important to ignore. Because of its location, the garden was highly visible to the world's power brokers, who passed by the bountiful rows of corn and zucchini every day.

A different example is in Denver, Colorado, where a nonprofit group called EarthLinks offers low-income and homeless people a chance to cultivate creativity. Through one of EarthLinks's programs, homeless people press the flowers they grow, then use them to decorate handmade candles and bookmarks. In the group's Peace Garden, homeless gardeners have demonstrated other aspects of their creativity. In one case, they carried a couch into the garden and, in the space normally occupied by the seat cushions, they planted a small crop of spuds, creating a literal translation of "couch potatoes."

In similar gardens across the country, beds are cultivated by people who want to develop new belief systems. This is part of the recovery and rebuilding process, to nourish themselves with new ideas, with new ways of being in the world. They change the world by changing their own minds about who they are.

Now *that's* a buffalo wallow.

Like my friend the prosecutor says, there's another world out there, one that we didn't make. As gardeners know, we can help it along, but in the end, it will give us more than we give it. It will nourish us. It will feed our souls.

h e a v e n
a n d   e a r t h

At the heart of gardening there is a belief in the miraculous.
—Mirabel Osler

Alabama defies all my northern prejudices. Driving in from Tennessee, I first thought the state looked just as expected. Long stretches of nothing but green marked the foothills of the Appalachians. Occasionally a new house appeared in view from the highway, but more frequently I saw off-kilter cabins built more than a century ago. From time to time, a curl of smoke lofted into the air from a burning trash pile. If that smoke happened to be in the proximity of a cabin, it looked just like a scene from an old hooked rug. It was just what I expected: rural, poor, parochial, a throwback to another time.

Then I drove into Huntsville.

Like all cities nowadays, Huntsville is skirted with fast-food restaurants, motel chains, and southern Waffle House restaurants thrown in for good measure. But downtown, the view changes. A historic district of elegant brick homes sits adjacent to a new trio of historical museums for children. They're not far from the 1819 Weeden

House Museum, which was built the same year that Alabama became a state. These, however, are not the attractions for which the community is best known. A city of southern heritage, Huntsville may be one of the few places in the South where Civil War–era history is preempted by outer space.

In 1952, Wernher von Braun moved to Huntsville to become technical director of the U.S. Army ballistic-weapons program. He and the entire German rocket team had surrendered to the United States after World War II, and they brought along some of the world's most advanced research in long-range missiles and rocketry. After *Sputnik 1* was launched by the Soviet Union in 1957, von Braun and his team launched *Explorer 1*, the first U.S. satellite, in 1958. Soon after, NASA was formed, and von Braun became director of the NASA George C. Marshall Space Flight Center in Huntsville.

Homer Hickam, the author of *October Sky* who, as a boy, was inspired by von Braun, lives in Huntsville. So do thousands of other engineers and high-tech professionals. In this city of 180,000, there are more people with doctorates than in all the rest of Alabama. One out of thirteen people is involved in the high-tech industry. Only 15 percent of the city's population is made up of Huntsville natives; the rest have come from all over the world, attracted by this miniature Silicon Valley–style settlement. You can find southern barbecue in Huntsville, but you can also find excellent Taiwanese. And the city has carved the country's second-largest research park out of cotton fields, replacing those fields with expanses of multi-million-dollar buildings and green spaces for employee picnics.

I've heard it said that in a city, the structure that stands tallest or on the promontory point is the one that represents what the city values most. In ancient cities, the tallest structures were cathedrals or pyramid-shaped temples. Today they're often financial centers. In Huntsville, the tallest structure is one you can see from miles away. Standing straight and tall, it is a replica of the *Saturn V* rocket, the spaceship that first took man to the moon.

❧

Jim Call is a technology guy. He works for a defense contractor and research company as an Internet analyst, following fifteen years as a computer programmer for Motorola. On the Friday when I went to visit him, he wasn't working behind a computer. Just as he does every Friday, he wears a pair of jeans, a T shirt with a CASA COMMUNITY GARDEN emblem, and a baseball cap. Fifty years old, he's a former long-distance runner, "like Forrest Gump," he says. One of his goals is to walk the Appalachian Trail, a course of 2,160 miles from Georgia to Maine. He is what you would probably call a type A personality. Yet he cut back his job to a thirty-two-hour workweek during the growing season so he could reserve Fridays for his true passion: running a garden program that's as far from high speed and high tech as they come.

We're pulling into the driveway at a small brick ranch house, the home of a woman whom Jim affectionately addresses in the proper southern way, with a unique blend of respect and familiarity. She is Miss Edith, and she is Jim's GardenFriend. Jim, in turn, is her GardenAngel.

"She's about seventy-four years old," Jim tells me, "and she's homebound. She had polio when she was young." Miss Edith worked as a nurse at the hospital three blocks away, walking to work every day for thirty years. Now, Jim says, she lives on $452 a month.

Jim knocks on the door, and through the screen we see Miss Edith making her way toward us with her walker, accessorized with a wicker basket on the front. Her gray hair is gathered up in a bun, and she wears a blue blouse and shorts in anticipation of the ninety-degree heat later in the day. Her white socks are rolled down around her ankles, and she wears a brace on one leg.

"How you doin', Miss Edith?" Jim says with his Georgia drawl.

"Just fine, just fine," she says. Her voice is high-pitched and a bit breathless. She is clearly delighted to see Jim.

This is planting day at Miss Edith's house. Jim has brought seedlings and garden tools, and within an hour, he will have a garden planted to give Miss Edith plenty of fresh produce to eat, probably enough to share. This is a program that Jim designed several years ago under the auspices of a local agency known as Care Assurance System for the Aging and Homebound, or CASA for short. Jim's program is called GardenAngel, a name that came to him in a dream.

"I was sleeping on the sofa," he says. "I do that a lot because I'm a very light sleeper, and if I can't sleep, I'll go to the couch. I was thinking about this program before I went to sleep, but I didn't have all the pieces of it put together yet. When I woke up, the name GardenAngel came to me, and I thought, that's *it*. After I had the name, everything else fell into place."

GardenAngel sounds a lot like guardian angel, Jim says, and that's the whole point. Through this program, volunteers from Huntsville are matched with elderly and homebound people. In the spring, the volunteers, or GardenAngels, plant a four-by-eight-foot garden for their GardenFriend. Then they come back eight or ten times during the growing season to check in.

The GardenFriend waters the garden and harvests it. But there's more going on here than tending the plants. The volunteers are the eyes and ears of CASA, which offers other services to the elderly and homebound. If a GardenFriend needs an air conditioning unit or fan, a roof repair or new paint job, the Angel reports back. "A lot of the elderly people are too proud to ask for help," Jim says. "The Angels don't have to do the work. They just let us know what people need."

Even this is not the greatest by-product of the GardenAngel program. That honor is reserved for companionship. "You build friendships and relationships with these people," Jim says. For Miss Edith, the friendship has introduced her to a whole new world.

❧

Despite his mustache, Jim has a kidlike quality about him, like a Mouseketeer who still brings the ears out for special occasions. He talks nonstop, smiles a lot, and knows how to tease. Jim keeps heading to the backyard to prepare for planting, then he pops back into the living room like a yo-yo on a string. There's one more thing to tell us, one more prompt for Miss Edith. They are talking about Miss Edith's favorite sites on the Internet.

"I like Egyptian pyramids," she says, her speech just a bit slurred, "and I like Jane Goodall, too. Her site is one of my favorites."

I'm in awe. Here's Miss Edith, so tiny she all but disappears in her recliner, and she is a fountain of knowledge about surfing the Web. It's all because of Jim.

"The first couple of times I came to see her," Jim says, "she asked me, 'What's this Internet thing?'"

She kept asking, and this is what Jim told her: "Just imagine walking into a huge library with a science room. And guess what, Miss Edith, it's so huge you could never read everything in it. That's the Internet." She probably smiled her childlike smile, so youthful you could almost expect her to clap her hands in glee. And before long, Jim brought her a surplus computer. But there was only one problem: Miss Edith couldn't type. The polio had impeded the mobility of her hands, and she'd gone her whole life without working at a keyboard.

Using her left hand, which works better than her right, she started pecking at the keys. Jim taught her how to use a mouse and acquainted her with a few basic computer tasks, and with his help, Miss Edith ventured online. Jim installed a program to enlarge the words, making it easier to read.

"The first week I got tired," Miss Edith says, looking out from her big chair. "I prayed about it a lot."

Before long, she had her own AOL account and was bookmarking Web sites for *National Geographic* daily news sites.

Lately, Jim has been downloading audio books onto CDs so Miss Edith can play them on her computer. Her favorites are by Danielle Steel and John Grisham. She plays Free Cell solitaire, receives pictures of her son and his family from New Mexico in PDF files, and goes places she never dreamed about. She is such a frequent Internet traveler, in fact, that every once in a while she'll receive an instant message from Jim. "Get off the computer," it will say. "I need to call you."

Miss Edith used to plant flowers, but now she lets Jim do that for her. She has a new way to stay connected to the planet.

"I didn't know beans about computers," Miss Edith says, "but it means the world to me now. I tell people you can take away my stove or TV, but don't take away my computer."

Jim's dad was a gardener. A retired sergeant, he had five children to raise, so he relied on the produce he grew to help feed the family. In his last year of life, he picked produce from his garden, put it in a paper sack, and took it to the ladies at the Waffle House restaurant where he often ate.

In Jim's younger years, gardening didn't make much of an impression. "At twelve years old, I could never understand why my dad wanted me to take a picture of him standing next to some tomatoes," he says. Even today, Jim doesn't consider himself much of a gardener, but he's put a lot of thought into the beds the GardenAngels plant for their Friends.

The gardens are ingenious in their simplicity. "Most of the GardenAngels know nothing about gardening. They're the sons and daughters of engineers," Jim says, as though that's all the explanation you need.

The raised beds start with a four-by-eight-foot rectangular frame built from western cedar landscape timbers. The frame is filled with topsoil and manure. On one long side, electrical conduit and PVC joints form an upright frame for growing pole beans. To guide the climbing vines, Jim cuts lengths of baling twine and ties them to the horizontal conduit, then pulls them straight down to the bed, where he has driven fencing staples in the landscape timber below. He ties the bottom of each string to a staple, then duct-tapes the tied string to the conduit so it won't shift. A dozen strings later, the pole beans have plenty of room to climb and grow.

Jim talks as he works, having done this so many times he can cut and tie in his sleep. Miss Edith and I are sitting in the shade in painted metal lawn chairs that Jim positioned for us out of the sun. He has thought about more than how to build these gardens, he said. He's thought a lot about the people they serve.

"Have you watched *Saving Private Ryan* or *Pearl Harbor*?" he asks. "They're about these people, these people we're helping. It's like Tom Brokaw's book says, this is America's greatest generation." He's cutting more lengths of baling twine and tying them in place.

"They grew up through the Depression," he says. "We've never experienced what it takes to eat nothing but apples for meals, right, Miss Edith?" He tears off little pieces of duct tape and wraps them over the knotted strings at the top.

"This country owes them a lot. When those people were growing up, there was no TV or computer. They'd sit outside and talk to each other: 'How's your garden doin' this year?' That was their entertainment."

Jim has thought through it all. Each garden is situated north to south so it will get full sun throughout the day, and so the climbing pole beans won't shade out the other plants. Normally, each garden includes tomatoes, beans, okra, and squash, although it can be altered a bit to suit the individual requests of each GardenFriend.

The planting package includes tomato cages, slightly composted leaves for mulch, and all the plants, donated by a local nursery. And that means *all* of them. "One year a cold wave came through, and we lost seventy percent of what we'd planted," Jim says. "They gave us all new plants."

Jim sets up the original gardens, building the frames and conduit units. Then, year after year, the Angels come and plant the gardens within the frames. It's as slick an operation as any NASA launch, and it takes less than an hour to do.

It is so well organized, in fact, that a few years ago Jim put together a materials list that spells out the plans. The list includes everything, down to the number of galvanized decking screws and staples and the Liquid Nails glue used to cement the PVC connection. The last item on the list is a bit unexpected.

"One five-foot boy, mischievous, twelve years old," it reads. Above it is a picture of Jim's youngest son standing next to the garden. In all probability, it looks a whole lot like Jim did thirty-eight years ago, snapping a photo of his dad with tomato plants at his side.

This is a model of the future, it seems: a high-technology world in which personal connections are more vital than ever. Apparently the people of Huntsville think so, too, because volunteerism is part of the culture here, with a high percentage of corporate employees donating their time to a variety of nonprofit programs. Jean Lee is one of the GardenAngels and, in fact, helped Jim get the program off the ground. She and her husband both worked for NASA for more than thirty years; her office was down the hall from von Braun's. In the seven years since she retired from her job as a budget analyst, she has treated volunteer work as her job. Jean serves on the board of both CASA and the Huntsville Botanical Garden, and she's currently the state vice president for the Master Gardeners program.

Jean grew up in a small town in Alabama, yet through her work she had the chance to travel the world, witness thirty shuttle launches, befriend the men who went into space, and experience the thrill of seeing President Kennedy waving to the crowd from his motorcade when he visited Huntsville early in the race to the moon. She was a part of the team through the best and worst of it all, celebrating when U.S. astronauts took their first steps on the moon's surface, and grieving with the rest of the staff years later when the explosion of the *Challenger* plunged the space program into darkness and self-doubt.

Looking at the whole of her career, Jean says, "I was at NASA at the right time." But now she has other things to do. On this blazing-hot afternoon, she is dressed in denim shorts, white sandals, and an embroidered blue-and-white-striped shirt that looks fresh and well pressed. We are on our way to see Miss Bessie, Jean's ninety-year-old GardenFriend. Jean says that Miss Bessie's positive attitude is the reason she's still able to live on her own. "Her favorite phrase is 'Thanks a million,'" Jean says. "She says that all the time."

Like Miss Edith, Miss Bessie is at the front door to greet us. She lives thirty minutes north of Huntsville, in an area that saw plenty of action during the Civil War, Jean says. Her front porch is cool and shady, with wooden rockers and a porch swing, all painted shiny green. The porch looks out over a field across the road and the mountains in the distance. "Look what I brought you, Miss Bessie," Jean says, getting out of the car. She hands Miss Bessie a jar of blackberry jelly with the seeds still in it, Miss Bessie's favorite.

"Why, thanks a million," Miss Bessie says.

Inside the house, the paneled front room is decorated with venetian blinds, lace curtains, and a shelf with knick-knacks hanging above an easy chair. Miss Bessie is just as Jean described. She is trim and crisp, with her white hair newly cut short. The afternoon has turned hot, but she looks cool and relaxed. She sits backboard-straight in her chair, which is covered by a blue-and-white printed afghan, and clutches a tissue in one hand. Her gestures are birdlike, her voice delicate but strong. Just like Jim and Miss Edith, there is a connection between Jean and Miss Bessie.

"How long have I been your GardenAngel, Miss Bessie?" Jean asks.

"I don't know," Miss Bessie says. "A long time. Four or five years. A long time."

In Miss Bessie's lifetime, she has buried two husbands and a son, worked in the cotton fields, and taken care of a daughter with special needs. Through it all, she grew plots of vegetables and "canned, canned, canned." She may not be able to plant her own garden anymore, but she still tends the one Jean plants for her. "If you find me dead in the garden," she says, "you'll know I died happy."

The two trade small talk. Miss Bessie has been feeling good, but her window air conditioner isn't working right. The tomatoes are doing well, on their way to meeting the July 4 ripening deadline that, in Alabama, proves you're a competent gardener. Her nephew is going to come mow the lawn tonight. And when he does, Miss Bessie will drag out the hose and water the garden. "I can do things if I have something to hold onto," she says. "If I can get a hold of a rake, I can do as much as anybody."

The GardenAngel raised bed is located where the old barn used to be, in a site where nutrients from cow manure kept the garden thriving the first several years. "The first year we planted green beans, you could stand there and watch 'em grow," Miss Bessie says.

This year's garden is growing, too, although Jean had to replant okra felled by the early heat. She puts compost on the bed while Miss Bessie watches from the back porch. Outbuildings and the entrance to a storm cellar surround the site. Four old large wash pans hang on nails from the side of a shed. It's clear they're not there just for visual effect. "She's sure worked hard all her life," Jean says.

Jean and Miss Bessie have developed a close friendship through the GardenAngel program, and the trust between them is obvious. One time, Jean says, she came to Miss Bessie's house and was met with a question.

"Is *he* with you?" Miss Bessie asked, referring to Jean's husband, who sometimes comes along on the visits.

"No, Miss Bessie," Jean said. "He's not with me today."

"Well," Miss Bessie said, leaning on the kitchen counter, "I just took a fall and hurt my hip, and I wonder if you could look at it for me."

"Sure, Miss Bessie," Jean said, not knowing what would come next.

Right there and then, Jean says, Miss Bessie turned her back and dropped her drawers. "She dropped *everything*," Jean says.

"I didn't see any bruises, but I kind of poked around a little to make sure nothing was broken," Jean says.

"When I got home, I e-mailed Jim. I told him what happened, and then I said, 'I didn't realize this was part of the GardenAngel program.'"

He e-mailed back right away. "Oh, yes," his e-mail read. "It's in Chapter 7, Section 22 of the manual, under 'Butt-Checking Your GardenFriend.'"

✦

Overseeing the GardenAngel program is just one of Jim's responsibilities. He also spends time directing the half-acre CASA Community Garden, which has just been moved to a new location. The site sits up on a hill on a busy thoroughfare in an area of the city that's highly visible for other reasons. It is adjacent to the Huntsville Botanical Garden, which is funded with private and corporate donations. And beyond that is the Space and Rocket Museum, a tribute to von Braun and the entire space program.

The CASA Community Garden operates on a much

larger scale than GardenAngel, which, because it's based on one-to-one relationships, serves just a handful of elderly residents a year. If Jim didn't have the responsibility of the community garden, he'd spend more time rustling up GardenAngel volunteers. "I don't have enough bandwidth to do it," he says.

It's easy to see why. The community garden provides fresh produce for more than 7,500 elderly people in Huntsville and throughout the county, with volunteers delivering it directly to the community rooms of retirement facilities and apartment complexes.

Both the city and county want this garden to set the standard for the nation, so they're willing to invest. The county commission donated funds to buy a six-foot-high fence surrounding the garden. In turn, the city is footing part of the $110,000 bill for moving the garden to its new location. It's also supporting CASA in its fund-raising efforts to finance a pavilion, gazebo, restrooms, and orchard. It may even dress up the entrance to the garden with a scarecrow that lights up at night.

If it does, it will be building on the garden's existing scarecrow motif. Schoolchildren made a couple dozen of them, guided by a heroes theme. One looks like an astronaut, one is a firefighter, another is a soldier. Guarding the ends of the rows of vegetables, they stand about eight feet high and are supported by cross beams that stick out from their arms. Unfortunately, there's just one little problem. "They look like they're being crucified," a neighbor complained. Jim isn't arguing. "Well, I can see what she means," he says. Some of the heads *are* flopping a bit, and the crossbeams stick out farther than they might. "I'll have to prop them up and cut off the ends of the beams,"

Jim says. How many people, I wonder, would complain about the complaint? This is one of the reasons Jim gets things done. He's patient, and he's willing.

On this Friday afternoon, he'll be at the garden starting at two P.M., learning how to use a trencher. "I never dreamed we'd be planting a garden with one of those," he says. But the soil in the garden is compacted and won't drain properly. The plants are showing signs of duress. So Jim and one of his half-dozen garden "mules" ("they're the volunteers who do all the hard and dirty work," Jim says) are going to dig trenches between the rows so the soil can drain. It's a temporary fix, just for this year. Jim will be there this afternoon in the heat, and he'll be there at six o'clock Saturday morning.

Jim and his mules direct the other volunteers, the ones who harvest the garden and do light garden maintenance. They will probably number 1,500 by the time this growing season is over. They come from churches, corporations, and civic groups. Even members of Mensa, the organization for people with an IQ higher than the national debt, have volunteered. "One guy came out last year," Jim says. "He'd never worn a pair of work gloves in his life, but he could draw a heck of a math equation on the chalkboard." Jim finds gardening tasks for all of them, no matter what their level of experience. He ices down bottles of water to keep them cool. And when they're done, he takes their picture with a digital camera and posts it on the community garden Web site that night. Sometimes the volunteers want Jim to get in the picture with them. "I tell them I can't because I'm wanted in seven states," he says with his Mouseketeer smile.

His job is 50 percent gardening, 50 percent logistics

with the volunteers. But he tells them, "If you don't come back next year, I haven't done my job.

"According to the mules, the number one rule in this garden," Jim says, "is that it's always the director's fault."

❧

A couple of years ago, Jim was on a cruise with his wife, celebrating their twenty-fifth wedding anniversary. One of the regular volunteers, Bob Molenda, saw that the plants in the community garden needed to be fertilized. He went into the shed, found the sprayer, and treated the entire garden. He didn't know that the sprayer was filled with defoliant instead of fertilizer.

When the peppers started to die and the tomatoes lost their leaves, the mules discovered what had happened, but no one knew what to do. Someone suggested calling Jim. "Don't do that," another said. "He'll jump off the boat and swim to shore." Instead, they washed down the garden and started to replant.

When Jim returned several days later, Bob was beside himself. "All these elderly people depend on this garden," he said, "and I've let them down."

Jim's response was immediate. "You just made a mistake," he said. "We all make mistakes, that's what life's all about. We'll get through this together." And they did. The garden still bore a record harvest of 6,309 pounds of tomatoes alone that year.

A few months after that happened, Bob suffered a fatal heart attack. Jim arranged for a memorial; a mural of Bob and another long-standing volunteer, Kent Haisten, who was Jim's garden mentor, is painted on a wall at the community garden.

The loss of Bob, and of Kent the year before, were two of the toughest challenges Jim has faced, tougher by far than the hardpan soil and drainage problem of the new community garden. In anticipation of a lighter yield, CASA has asked local garden clubs to plant a row for the less fortunate, with the produce to be donated to CASA for their regular distribution. Jim's apologetic about it, but he knows it's just another minor snag in the whole scheme of things. Economically, this garden is a no-lose proposition. "It costs less than $1,000 a year to run the program," Jim says, "and last year we gave away more than $20,000 worth of produce."

Standing in the company of the scarecrows with poor posture, we look out over the garden. It's a pretty spot, higher than much of the land around it, with an expansive view. You can see for a long way, off to the east at the Botanical Center, and at the Space and Rocket Museum beyond. There it is, the *Saturn V*, looming in the distance as a reminder of man's ability to explore other worlds. But this garden, these scarecrows, the mural of Bob and Kent—they bring you back to earth, ground you in what's real and enduring.

Jim nods toward the rocket, silhouetted against the sky. "Look at that," he says. "That's high tech, and this is high heart. Everything we do impacts humanity."

greetings
from rocky roost

"Just living is not enough," said the butterfly. "One must
have freedom, sunshine, and a little flower."
—Hans Christian Andersen

Pierce Williams woke up with a red eye this morning.
It looks like a touch of conjunctivitis, accompanied by
a bit of crankiness, so he won't be gardening today. He
walks around in his red clog-style slippers, though, and
after a while he's energetic enough to go out in the yard
and jump up and down on his Air Pogo, which is just the
right size for a three-year-old.

Meanwhile, Pierce's mom, Julie, is feeding Garrett,
the eight-month-old and youngest of three boys. This
could be a typical family scene: Dad is off at the office, big
brother Jake is at school, and Mom and the two younger
boys are spending the day at home. But this is no ordinary
household. This is a place where indoors and out, as well
as reality and fantasy, are indistinguishable one from the
other. Like a character in a children's book, this home even
has a name: Rocky Roost, inspired by its setting in the side
of a mountain on the outskirts of Hot Springs, Arkansas.

The house has a touch of Dr. Seuss about it. The boards are a bit crooked and the roof tips cockeyed, and you might expect Horace and a Who to come whipping around the corner or sliding down the fall of water that trickles down the mountain and then shunts into a stream flowing right by the kitchen door. Salamanders skittered under the corner of that door until Julie and her husband, Jim, plugged it up. But the salamanders are still around, like slithery reminders that there's a natural balance within these wild parameters of mountain, woods, and fence. There are, by the way, also snakes and broad-headed skinks on the property, along with a wide assortment of other critters.

But really, who *wouldn't* like it here? Julie's an artist who names her furniture. Jim's a lawyer who wants to build a Bubba Shack up on the mountain as his own private getaway. And the three boys . . . well, they don't know who they are yet. But that's the whole point. This is an excellent place to find out.

✧

First, you have to picture Rocky Roost because you probably haven't seen anything quite like it. The house is separated from an unpaved road by narrow garden beds, an unpainted picket fence, an old iron gate, and an arbor covered with rambling roses. The house resembles an old coal-miner's cabin, all ramshackle and stone, with a copper chimney and a tin-covered porch held up by two posts—one right side up and the other upside down. Its condition is partly due to age and gravity, and partly to Julie's affinity for what she calls "rustic opulence." This means that the front porch is furnished with an old wooden wheelbarrow, peeling-paint tables, child-sized chairs, collections of rocks, and wire hanging baskets. We may be in Arkansas, but this is not hillbilly decorating. It is, like California shabby chic, a way to decorate with creativity instead of a checkbook.

To the side of the house is the patio, garden, and play space, all rolled into one. That's where the Air Pogo hangs from a tree near a plastic castle, which sits right next to the Wonder horse and a sandbox with bamboo poles sticking out in the form of a teepee. There's plenty of mulch filling the space up to the terraced garden, where stacks of bricks mark the border. Loosely arranged stones lead through the garden, a collection of geraniums, sedum, hostas, and ivies. And just beyond that is the base of North Mountain, where the garden suddenly becomes a thicket of underbrush and trees.

Across the open space, probably forty feet from the house, is the Opera House, a newly built guest house/art studio made with rusty nails and old boards to match the Ozark character of Rocky Roost. It's decorated with miscellany and architectural salvage, a subcategory of rustic opulence that Julie has named "yard flotsam." This unique decorating genre includes broken rocking chairs found by the side of the road, chunks of marble resting in a birdbath, and a little wishing well that sits on the Opera House's front porch.

Inside the main house, Julie is curled up in an oversized chair in the living room, nursing Garrett, talking about the total environment the family has created. The fireplace is a mass of stone, over which hangs a decorative piece of molding from an old bedstead. Across the room hang Julie's paintings of chili peppers and the bathhouses for which Hot Springs is known. Julie, in a lime green linen shirt and black pants, is a red-headed blend of energy, creativity, and calm.

We can smell the sweetness of the bark mulch outside, and we can hear the sound of the cold spring water coming off the mountain. Because the house literally backs into North Mountain, water that flows next to the house directs itself properly into the kitchen side stream. Other times it gets out of hand and misbehaves, cascading into a closet at the back of the house. When Pierce was eighteen months old, the community experienced torrential rain. When it ceased, the water in the closet dried up. One day Julie noticed Pierce carrying cups of water to the back of the house.

"What are you doing?" she asked him.

"Watering the closet," he said.

Someday, Julie says, she and Jim are going to fix that little problem. But there's no particular hurry. As long as the leaking closets inspire the kids to think, solve, explore, troubleshoot, and imagine, then they're fine just the way they are.

❧

If the story of Rocky Roost were a children's book, the kids would be illustrated wearing pith helmets and Eddie Bauer hiking boots, using magnifying glasses to look under rocks, examine the texture of the lamb's ears in the garden, and study the best way to slide down a boulder that's bigger than their plastic castle.

Rocky Roost is, in fact, like a fascinating observable universe, all unto itself. There are many things to learn from this place, but a few of them are these: why fresh air is better than video games, how to plant a garden in a wheelbarrow, the proper placement of the plastic dinosaur among flowers and foliage, and why a little imperfection is absolutely perfect, especially where flowers and kids are concerned. If we were to write a Rocky Roost primer on letting plants and children bloom wherever they are, here are a few of the things it might say.

Remember Julie's foxglove. Julie's been passing on a love of gardening to her boys ever since Jake was a toddler. She does this by giving them the tools and opportunities to discover the wonder and beauty of the garden on their own terms. A small wheelbarrow is just the right size for Pierce. So are kid-sized garden tools and gloves. Julie buys several pairs of gloves for the boys. "It's okay to wear them mismatched," she says.

An old rusted regular-sized wheelbarrow filled with dirt is a miniature garden in itself. Julie, Jake, and Pierce planted it with rows of lettuce, basil, and spinach. Near the wheelbarrow, Pierce points out a single lamb's ear that's poking its way out between two bricks in the garden terrace. Its color is the same as the dusty miller, which Pierce likes because of its name.

Julie inherited a passion for gardening from her mom. "When I was little, she took me to the nursery and let me pick out a flower," Julie says. "It was a foxglove, and I still remember it clearly. I thought it was the most amazing, beautiful thing I ever saw."

This is why Julie now takes her boys to the nursery and lets them pick out whatever they like, even if it's not what she would choose. It's also why Julie doesn't worry about any particular color scheme in the garden. As with the water in the closets, you have to keep things in perspective.

⌒

Combine gardening with art. They're both tactile, and they both give kids the chance to express themselves, to create something that they can look at and say, "That's me." As an artist, Julie possesses a strong sense of what looks good and what doesn't, but as a mom, she knows perfection can be overrated.

"I've seen parents bring their daughter to art class wearing a perfect little dress, and if she gets a drop of paint on it, the mom goes crazy," Julie says. That would not happen here. Here the boys have their own child-sized worktable out in the garden, where they draw and make their own brand of art.

Pierce has a sculpture that's a work in progress. It's about eighteen inches tall, with a frame made from a tripod of twigs. At Easter, he added an egg-shaped maraca painted with stripes. Sparkly star tinsel and beads are wrapped all around the sculpture, making it look a little like a rocket ship decorated for a Mardi Gras parade. While it was made in the garden and today sits in the garden, it travels around Rocky Roost. It has been featured in the middle of the living room table and as a birthday centerpiece, surrounded by a collection of rocks. Someday it may end up in the sculpture garden Julie hopes to create in the lot on the other side of the house. She'll use old pieces of iron to make easels for her artwork, and Pierce's rocket could be displayed under a tree somewhere. Maybe it will be labeled PIERCE WILLIAMS: EARLY PERIOD.

Forget "mistakes." Go for magic. Julie has written a couple of stories and illustrated them for the boys. One is *The Octopus's Garden*, which tells the story of how octopuses gather shiny objects—sea flotsam, if you will—and make their own cache on the ocean floor. It's an entertaining and absolutely true piece of marine biology trivia, Julie says, and she's included supportive material at the end as evidence. One page shows the octopus with a photocopy of a shiny penny.

The other book is *Jake and the Pumpkin*, also based on a true story. When Jake was Pierce's age, he and his mom planted flowers and vegetables from seed. Jake had his heart set on pumpkins, but Julie thought they didn't have enough room. In a few weeks, a pumpkin vine appeared in a small bed near the road, and Jake admitted to planting the seed on his own. Pumpkins have been a staple at Rocky Roost ever since. "We have so many that they deflate and we scoop them away," Julie says. Next year, she will move the plants into the terraced garden, where there's more room for them to spread. But for now, they front a wall that Julie painted several shades of rust, giving it a weathered appearance. While she was painting, a man walked by, looked at it, and said with concern, "Did you know it's not all the same color?"

"Yes," Julie said. "I meant to do it that way."

The man looked scared and ran, Julie said.

Buy a rubber snake. Just as pumpkins have played a major role at Rocky Roost, so has a rubber snake from

Booger Hollow. Down the road from Count Razorback's Liar's Headquarters and Bait Shop, Booger Hollow is a gift store and restaurant for tourists. It sits along Highway 7, which leads from Eureka Springs to Hot Springs. The road winds through Ozark National Forest and makes you think of two things: First, that this is the closest you can come to taking a roller coaster ride in a Dodge Caravan. And second, that if you're going to live in Arkansas, you have to really like it because it's not easy to get in or out.

At Booger Hollow, the Williams family bought a rubber snake for Jake. For a time, it overlooked a volcano that Jake built in the garden sandbox, topped with the bamboo teepee and covered with a tarp. The snake was wrapped around the bamboo, where from time to time it witnessed simulated volcanic eruptions.

The snake also played a role in a scavenger hunt that Julie and Jim arranged for Jake's birthday party. Not only did it turn the sandbox into a snake pit, but young guests had to look for clues near a pair of green shoes that were said to belong to an ogre, near a cauldron of dry ice tended by Jim in a bathrobe and sunglasses, and near a dragon's egg hidden in a feather boa in the loft of the Opera House. When the fire in the Opera House's woodstove smoldered a bit, the boys were all convinced that the smoke was coming from the mouth of the dragon.

~

Look for vocational clues. The Williamses have found crystals during hikes up the trails behind the house. "I worry about picking them up," Julie says. "I wonder what's going to power the earth if they're gone." But these crystals don't go far from their source. The Williamses and their friends deposit them in the stream and the gardens. In addition, a dozen of the little filmy-white monoliths are plunged into a block of floral oasis. They sit in the un-roofed shed outside the kitchen door, along with a potting table covered in chicken wire and a chandelier with teardrop-shaped crystals, much like the one hanging on the front porch.

There may be a few crystals in the leather satchel that sits on a table in the living room, surrounded by Julie's paintings. That satchel holds Jake's collection of natural wonders, and even Julie doesn't know what's in it. It's safe to guess that there are rocks and fossils. This is because Jake likes to dig. At the age of three, he told everyone he knew that he wanted to be a paleontologist. When he announced this to strangers, they'd sometimes ask him what that was. He'd look at them quizzically, studying their ignorance, and inform them, "It's someone who digs for dinosaur bones and eggs."

"He dug and dug one year," Julie says, "but he couldn't find any bones. He was so disappointed."

He's found ways to cope. This Mother's Day, he and his dad went downtown to a fossil shop and he bought his mom a mounted fossil. Being his mother's son, he also bought the little rusted iron stand on which it was displayed.

"He did good," Julie says.

◆

Turn the world into your garden. There may be a fence on one side of Rocky Roost and a mountain on the other, but there's not much sense in letting boundaries get in your way. The Williamses would tell you to explore beyond the garden. Plant stuff on the other side of the fence. Scale the mountain even if you *are* pregnant and pushing a stroller.

The entire family and many friends have made those excursions up the mountain, ducking under and around the thickets of trees. Jake is yet to find dinosaur bones, but he has found shards of Native American pottery on the old trails. And several times, he's heard some great stories in Story Valley.

Here, Julie says, they all sit on a big boulder on a bed of pine needles and moss, and they tell tales. "Mainly about nice ogres," she says. Or about Mr. Red Rump (who is, thankfully, a chipmunk) and the Snake. Or about Jake's Mountain, a series of stories about a little boy who climbs a mountain and can have anything he wants because of his magical powers.

Story Valley has powers of its own. Once known as the Valley of the Vapors, it was a source of novaculite, a white rock that Native Americans in the area traded to the many Indians who visited the valley. It was used to make arrowheads. Julie thinks the Native Americans liked the white rock because if they shot an arrow and it missed its target, it would be easier to find. "And anyway, a quiver of them would look cool," she says.

In any event, the trees and hikes and magical powers clearly have influenced Jake. This is what allowed him, at age seven, to respond to his schoolteacher's Presidents' Day question of, "If you were president, what would you do?"

Without deliberation, he stood in front of his classmates and announced, "If I were president, I would stop them from cutting down all the trees."

Turn the garden into your world. At Rocky Roost, the garden is not minimized into a place to weed. It's more a place where you do outrageous things that don't seem too outrageous because everybody's having too good a time. It probably started with Jim and Julie's Cajun wedding anniversary party, which horrified a good friend. The friend could cope with the watering cans and birdhouses used as decorations on the tables, but she balked at the mule rides. And just to aggravate her a bit more, Julie recorded the *Beverly Hillbillies* and *Deliverance* theme songs and played them at strategic moments during the party.

At night, the garden might still look like it's ready for a reception, since it's illuminated with white Christmas lights strung up over a wire arbor. The lights extend the children's playtime and make it easier to see real snakes. On a big table sits a piece of flotsam, a metal tray with a pipe leading from one end. It was probably part of an air-conditioning unit, but Julie filled it with rocks, moss, and a small garden sculpture and used it as the centerpiece for a neighborhood progressive Christmas dinner.

There's a wire dressmaker's form standing in the garden. It was a gift from Julie's mom, who was understandably scared to see where it would end up. A carved bear sits on the porch of the Opera House, next to a birdhouse made of gnarled wood that looks like it could house trolls from the Ozark National Forest. And in the front yard sits a three-foot-diameter boulder that Jim gave Julie for Christmas a few years ago. Renting a backhoe on Christmas Eve to move the rock to their house was a bit of a trick, but they got the job done. Julie likes it because it has a climbing ramp, a spot that makes it easy for the boys to hoist themselves up and slide.

Trust the innate wisdom of nature and children. The house may be crooked, and the salamanders may sneak into the kitchen from time to time, but everything is in natural order at Rocky Roost. When a storm felled the wisteria vines a couple of years ago, Julie and the kids were devastated at first. The vines had been so thick that, when the blooms fell, they called it lavender snow. But within a few weeks, with the vines still twisted and lying on the ground after the storm, the wisteria bloomed more profusely than ever. "Nature fixed itself," Julie says.

This could be said for raising children, too. Give them nurturing and space to ramble and climb, and they'll find their place and thrive. Julie points out a metal painted rooster in the garden. Trying to find the right spot for it presented a yard-flotsam dilemma. She put it everywhere: on the steps of the Opera House, down by the fence, near the dress form. But it never looked right. So she handed it to Pierce and said, "Find a good spot for this." And he did.

"Look where he put it," Julie says, pointing. There it sits, where only a three-year-old would know it belonged: On a rock, overlooking the sedum plants known as Hens and Chicks.

Pierce is feeling better, having forgotten the irritation of his pinkeye. He's pushing Garrett in the swing on the

Opera House porch, surveying all he's created. Soon, there will be fruit hanging from the vines in the strawberry pot he helped plant, and one of these days, he and his brothers just may dig deep enough to find a few dinosaur bones.

It brings to mind Julie's favorite verse from *Jake and the Pumpkin*:

"Children should garden, don't you see?
That's why it's called a nursery."

Rocky Roost is a bit like *The Hardy Boys and the Mystery of North Mountain* come to life. If part of making a difference in the world is giving kids the imaginative space and freedom to discover who they are, then this is that place.

Julie plans to plant ginkgo trees because they're prehistoric and will suit Jake's fascination with the ancient. Pierce has yet to express a vocational interest, but he's currently helping build a rock wall out beyond the fence. And Garrett, who is too young even for garden clogs, nonetheless is showing signs of following in his older brothers' footsteps; any chance he gets, he goes after the potted palms on the front porch.

The fun of raising kids, it seems, is helping them try on different ideas of themselves to see how they fit. They may wear some ideas for a while, then shed them like a snake's skin. Other ideas may be a fit for life. It's like a scavenger hunt in the garden, looking for clues, creating new expressions of yourself, paying attention to your favorite plants, climbing rocks, telling stories—all in that rootedness you have when you've been given the gift of home.

remembering

Oh, this is the joy of the rose—that it blooms and goes.
—Willa Cather

I picked up the book *Wilfrid Gordon McDonald Partridge* the other day on the recommendation of Diane Shaw, an elementary school teacher in Worth County, Georgia. She mentioned it because she reads it to her classes, sometimes while they sit outside in the Memory Garden behind the school. It's back there in what they call The Lamb's Yard, which is the name given to several gardens built by the teachers, staff, and students, who are in kindergarten through second grade.

Wilfrid Gordon McDonald Partridge, written by Mem Fox, is the story of a boy who befriends an elderly woman named Miss Nancy Alison Delacourt Cooper, whom he likes because she has four names, too. Miss Nancy has lost her memory, and Wilfrid helps her find it again. I mention *Wilfrid* partly because it's a book worth reading, and partly because it's the intersecting point between the Memory Garden at Worth County Primary School and the Portland Memory Garden at a park in Oregon. The first is a tribute to lost loved ones, the second is a way to connect with loved ones whose memories are lost to

Alzheimer's. They are both reminders of the ways in which gardens create and spark memories for us, the many ways in which they tie us to loved ones who are still with us and those who have gone on. They nourish us in different ways by helping us to remember.

∽

Worth County Primary School in Sylvester, Georgia, opened in 1995 in a rural, economically depressed part of southwestern Georgia where, according to a couple of the teachers and the former principal, many of the kids don't have a lot of beauty in their lives. When the school opened, the setting was not especially beautiful, either. The building, a total of 128,000 square feet, sprawled out over acres of red Georgia clay. Some people say all the topsoil was buried underneath the school; others say it was loaded up and trucked away. In any event, the land around the new building was raw and exposed, with nothing to look at, and pretty soon, one thousand little kids were going to be walking through the school doors.

Worth Primary is an exceptional place for many reasons, including the fact that every kindergartener, first-grader, and second-grader in the county attends this school. This means there are twenty-one kindergarten classes, fifteen classes of first-graders, and fifteen of second-graders, all wide-eyed and ready to soak up ideas in their spongelike brains. But you can just imagine how intimidating it would be if you were scarcely three feet tall and you walked into a building that, relative to your size, probably seems the equivalent of several football fields, with twists and turns and hallways and classrooms and lots and lots of doors.

Julie Sumner, the now-retired first principal of Worth Primary, spent her career seeing life through the eyes of children, and she had an idea. What if, she thought, they named every hallway in the school, just like a little community? The idea led to hallways with names like Watermelon Way and Fuzzy Bear Freeway, with child-sized street signs marking the intersections. But then, since they had a map of the community, there was no reason not to have a postal service within the school. So at Julie's request, Diane and many staff members developed the Wee Deliver program, which gives 120 kids a year experience as Worth Primary postal workers.

The students take a postal exam, apply for a job, interview, and work in the school's post office. Each classroom has its own address and a mailbox outside the door, so the postal workers make morning and afternoon deliveries, carrying letters from classes on one side of the building to pen-pal classes on the other side. The letters carry one-cent stamps designed each year by students who submit their artwork for consideration. You can just imagine tiny kids with freckles and skinned knees walking through the hallways carrying their mail, making deliveries with their seven-year-old unadulterated pride.

Like Wee Deliver, Worth Primary's Outdoor Classroom Project has earned the school state and national recognition. This project includes a four-by-eight-foot garden next to each classroom, a five-acre nature trail with bird and squirrel feeders and concrete toadstools where kids can sit for minilectures as they walk through the woods adjacent to the school, and a twenty-thousand-square-foot garden that the kids named The Lamb's Yard.

The Lamb's Yard includes multiple themed gardens.

In the musical playscape, which is equivalent to a small outdoor theater, the students perform on a rain wheel, marimba, tongue drums, and metallophones, all designed by a local resident and built with the help of local high school students in a construction class.

The Storybook Garden contains a fairy area shaped like a wing, where a strawberry pot serves as an apartment complex for fairies. Jack's area includes enormous footprint steppingstones and a hyacinth bean tree. Observation windows provide a view of what happens underground in the Tops and Bottoms bed, while an herb area tempts the senses.

Among these spaces is the Memory Garden, which was dedicated in 2001. The idea for it came to Julie because, in the few short years since the school had opened, the staff and students had lost two colleagues and five children—an enormous and unexpected loss.

It was developed, like other garden projects, with the full involvement of the kids, because that's how Worth Primary is run. Mary Beth Cary is the Outdoor Classroom chairman. From the time the school opened, she was concerned about the fact that the hardpan clay around the school was inhospitable even to weeds. "We had no frogs, no bugs—it was awful," she says. "Our goal was to make it look nice and have it be a haven for two-, four-, six-, and eight-legged creatures."

To start the project, she read *Wilfrid Gordon McDonald Partridge* to the kids on the Outdoor Classroom Students' Advisory Council, then she asked them, "What is a memory?" Their answers, which demonstrate why we should listen to kids more often, included the following: happy thoughts; things that make you laugh; something you remember from long ago or a few minutes ago; something you love, that makes you sad, or is "stuck in the mind which will never come out." The children also made a list of the elements they wanted in the garden, like flowers, a sign, benches, shade, names of the people who died, and a blue fence.

So the staff, students, and parents got together on Saturday workdays and built the garden. They planted forget-me-nots, dianthus, and crepe myrtle—all pastel and serene, the kind of soft, airy plants that drift in the breeze like cares that blow away. Wrought-iron benches came from a regional manufacturer. And instead of a blue fence, they installed three corner fences that frame the thirty-by-fifty-foot garden like a photo in an old photo album. They also added angel steppingstones, emotion stones with happy and sad faces, an angel, and an arbor. Bricks are engraved with the names of the memorialized staff members and students.

For the dedication ceremony, the school invited the families of those who had died. "For every joy that passes, something beautiful remains," Julie said in the dedication statement. You can just imagine the little kids holding their parents' hands or supported in their arms, listening to all this, smelling the fragrance of the flowers, thinking about the meaning of it all in the ways kids do, when their eyes glaze over like they're submerged in deep water and see things we can't—like the fairies in a strawberry pot.

On that day, the school honored two staff members who had died of cancer. One was Mary Paulk, who had been one of the first kindergarten teachers in Georgia and, at Worth Primary, served on the Outdoor Classroom Committee. The other was Ann Bozeman, a paraprofessional who, in her last months, came to school in her wheelchair and helped out in the post office. A student drew a picture of her and submitted it as a stamp design for the school. "It was a remarkable likeness," Julie says. "It just gives me chills to think how children respond to people they know love and care about them."

The garden sits in the middle of The Lamb's Yard, where memories take their place in the heart of the garden. It's a place where you can go and reflect, Julie says, and look out and see life and activity. The teachers take kids out to the memory garden every once in a while, read *Wilfrid Gordon McDonald Partridge* to them, and talk about happy memories as well as sad ones. The garden instills a sense of stewardship in the children, says Mary Beth, and "a respect for life, no matter what form it takes."

On the other side of the country, at a park in Portland, Oregon, people also sit in a garden and talk about memories. This is a different population, though—not elementary school students and their teachers, but caregivers and elderly people with Alzheimer's. The Portland Memory Garden was dedicated almost a year to the day after the garden at Worth Primary. And like the garden in The Lamb's Yard, it was built with the help of many volunteers.

The Portland Memory Garden, in fact, is a model of gardens for people with Alzheimer's and also a testament to agencies and organizations working together. It started when the American Society of Landscape Architects set a goal for its centennial celebration in 1999 of building one hundred parks in one hundred cities across the country. In Portland, they were lucky to find leadership and enthusiasm from people like Eunice Noell-Waggoner of the Center of Design for an Aging Society; Teresia Hazen, a horticultural therapist with Legacy Health System; and members of the Oregon Trail Chapter of the Alzheimer's Association, Portland Parks & Recreation, and the Portland State University Institute on Aging/School of Urban Studies and Planning.

They, along with dozens of community volunteers, designed and built the gardens as a place where caregivers could bring people with Alzheimer's to sit and talk and enjoy the smell of flowers and a dose of natural light. Contrary to what most of us believe, seventy-five percent of people with Alzheimer's are cared for in the home by family members; only one-quarter of them are in special care facilities. As a result, the benefits to weary caregivers were considered along with those for the people with Alzheimer's.

The garden sits in Ed Benedict Park, which occupies seven city blocks in a low-income neighborhood. On one side are single-family homes and apartments; on the other side are commercial businesses. Soccer fields, basketball courts, and playground equipment take up one part of the park. But separate from those busy areas was an open area with trees where a garden could be installed.

This park in this neighborhood was deemed an ideal site by the people of Portland for several reasons. First, the land was flat, which would make it accessible to people with walkers and in wheelchairs. Second, it's close to several long-term care facilities for people with Alzheimer's, as well as "foster care" facilities, where up to five elderly people are given care in a homelike setting. And third, residents of the neighborhood lobbied for it. The desire for the garden was so great, in fact, that while it was still under construction, a woman brought her elderly mother to the park in a wheelchair and stood outside the fence watching. On the first day the park opened, she was there with her mother, eager to take advantage of the setting.

Designed specifically as an Alzheimer's memory garden, it encompasses several special elements. When you stand at the entrance, you can look out over the entire garden and get your bearings, an important first step for both caregivers and those with Alzheimer's. Once you enter the garden, you find yourself following wide paths that easily accommodate people using wheelchairs or walkers. Handrails along the flowerbeds are there to steady those with halting steps. And raised, sloping beds allow you to touch plants without bending over. A circular stone planter forms a focal point in the center of the garden, and everywhere you look are sensory stimuli, such as birdhouses, wind chimes, and bird feeders.

The garden is fenced, which is a blessing to both the caregivers and the people with Alzheimer's, who are at risk of wandering off in search of something familiar. Here, that can't happen. With a fence as part of the landscape, there is only one entrance or exit. This makes it easy for tired caregivers to take their loved ones or clients to the garden and allow them to walk around without being constantly by their side.

The plants themselves, of course, are a major draw. Because Portland doesn't experience severe winters, it's not dependent on the swell of summer for garden grandeur. In fact, plantings were designed for four-season sensory stimulation, from the fragrance of roses and lilacs to grasses that blow in the wind, leaves that rustle, and evergreens that are soft and fragrant in every season. Volunteers planted six hundred pansies for major winter color. And all the plants are nontoxic in case they're ingested, a relief to ever-vigilant caregivers.

Many of the plants, like hollyhocks and daffodils, are those that people with Alzheimer's might have known in their childhoods or planted themselves. This familiarity could spark a memory. But that's not the main point, says Teresia Hazen. "With some early-stage Alzheimer's clients, there may be some memory retrieval," she says, "but we're not counting on that."

Instead, the plantings create a place of beauty and respite, and opportunities for sensory experience. "Once you start losing your intellectual memory," Eunice says, "then you experience everything on a sensory level."

Nancy Chapman, an environmental psychologist who helped develop the garden, knows the value of the garden in another way: as a conversation starter. Her mother had Alzheimer's, and she knows how difficult it can be to visit someone who doesn't recognize you and has trouble verbalizing thoughts. She interviewed family members and staff at Alzheimer's residential facilities, and she found that they mentioned the same thing she had found: Taking a walk in a garden is a way of engaging a loved one, of seeing something that might spark some kind of exchange. A garden was a way of staying in touch.

"I would have to say that I tried gardening with my mother," Nancy says. "That just didn't work. But she could enjoy walking around and touching and smelling the plants." It was an added benefit that her mother had been a gardener. "So many people have done some level of gardening, men as well as women," Nancy says.

Anyone who sits in the garden is benefiting in a way that could easily be overlooked, yet is the focus of Eunice's work. Her background is in interior design for an aging population, with an emphasis on lighting. "People need to experience bright light levels to keep sleep activity cycles synchronized with day and night cycles of life," she says. For people with Alzheimer's who are often confined to homes or long-term care facilities, exposure to the outdoors can be minimal. This may disrupt their circadian rhythms, make it difficult for them to sleep, and contribute to the "sundowning" idea that people with Alzheimer's become agitated at night. And if they're disruptive at night, they interfere with the health of their families, making it more likely that they'll be placed in a residential facility instead of staying at home. In essence, then, time in a garden can improve the sleep and eating habits of people with Alzheimer's and contribute to their staying in the care of their loved ones.

The Portland Memory Garden is one of only two such gardens in public parks in the United States; the other is in Macon, Georgia. But Eunice, Teresia, Nancy, and the others involved are offering training sessions to help people in other parts of the country replicate their success. The garden can't restore the joy of shared memory, but it can create a place for lives to touch one another again.

∽

In *Wilfrid Gordon McDonald Partridge*, Miss Nancy wears a dress of many colors. She is lumpy like a comfortable old chair, and she wears pink socks that sag around her ankles and slippers that probably shuffle when she walks. Wilfrid helps her find her memory by bringing her a basket filled with items that spark remembrances, like a shell that transports her back to the beach of her girlhood, and a puppet that reminds her of a time when she made her younger sister laugh.

That's the miracle of memories. The littlest thing, like the faint whiff of a lilac, can take us back forty years in time and across hundreds of geographic miles, transcending time and space unaided by our will or intention.

The Portland Memory Garden may not trigger memories like Wilfrid does for Miss Nancy. But it will give caregivers a chance to create new memories while they can. And in the Worth Primary Memory Garden, a forget-me-not may assist in grieving the loss of a teacher, classmate, or loved one. In any event, those primary students know that a garden can help us with memories that are "stuck in the mind which will never come out."

It may be the call of a bird or the sway of a crepe myrtle branch that jogs our memories, freeing us to live now and revisit the past when we want. Maybe that's why memory gardens are so fitting, because they remind us of the changing cycles of life, of the rightness and ultimate emancipation of change, decline, loss, and rebirth. Just as the planets move in a pattern we did not create, so, too, the mystery of time, of space, and of memory unfolds, right under our feet.

gardens that unite

It was March of 1996, and I was in Guatemala with four other Iowans, taking part in a cultural exchange. We'd spent four weeks traveling through the mountains and to the sea, visiting urban businesses and remote Mayan villages, and staying in the homes of host families. By the end of our visit, we were exhausted, ready to pick up a few souvenirs in the market, and return home. But on the last day before we were to leave, we were invited to a party.

Isabel, our host, told us that the festivities were to be held at a coffee ranch owned by a woman named Doña María, a longtime family friend. The ranch was located outside Antigua, the former capital city that stands as a monument to the colonial era of the 1500s. It's a place that challenges your equilibrium, as many of the buildings have been shaken on their foundations by multiple earthquakes. Still, they stand with a curious and haunting kind of beauty, housing shops and businesses with broken facades and jagged edges exposed.

Antigua, like the rest of Guatemala, endured a thirty-year civil war that ended just two months before our visit. Guatemala is an incredibly complex country, equal in land size to North Dakota and in population to Michigan, yet partly populated by more than twenty-two groups of Mayans. Each group has its own dialect, its own mode of dress, and its own customs, effectively fragmenting the country like the architectural shards in Antigua. Since the time of Spanish colonization, the Mayans have been in conflict with wealthy landowners. Those landowners rely on the indigenous people to harvest their coffee fields, but they developed a form of indentured servitude, in which the Mayan families accumulated debt they could never repay.

The civil war that started in the 1960s raged for an entire generation, yet there were no bombed-out buildings or abandoned artillery. It had been fought in hand-to-hand combat, mostly in the mountains of central Guatemala, where thousands of men, women, and children became *desaparecidos*, the disappeared, who were rounded up at gunpoint and never seen again.

Visiting Guatemala on the heels of the peace treaty was like arriving after a play is over. The set was dismantled, the costumes laundered, and the discussion was done. The war receded into the past; today, a party beckoned. Doña María was hosting a celebration for her migrant workers on the last day of the coffee harvest. Isabel told us it was an annual event.

When we drove up the dirt road of the ranch, we saw Doña María with the Mayan workers, standing near a mariachi band. She was petite, dressed in a denim shirt, jeans, and a wide-brimmed straw hat, and she looked younger than her seventy years. We stood and watched for a few minutes while she helped serve the workers. She spoke to each one as she handed them a plate of tamales, crouched down to talk to the children eye to eye, and seemed sincere in her thanks for their help. When she was free, she welcomed us, and then invited us to look around the ranch.

The first stop was the dairy barn, where tile-roofed stalls surrounded a courtyard with a hexagonal drinking trough. Over each cow stanchion hung a delft nameplate bearing the name of that cow. Doña María, said Isabel, knew the name of each one.

We walked on to the house, a classic hacienda with rooms adjoining a long westward-facing porch. We sat in the dining room, admiring shelves of Mayan artifacts and an arrangement of flame-colored persimmon leaves on the fireplace mantel. A Mayan woman with long dark braids served us cake and tea. "She's worked for Doña María ever since I was little," Isabel said.

And then there was the garden. Enclosed by hedges and a rail fence, this was a patch of paradise, with tranquil ponds and heirloom roses brought from France a century ago by Doña María's grandmother. We walked the paths among lemon trees, orchids, calla lilies, and myrrh. We sat under arbors and rubbed our fingers on fragrant leaves. And we admired the gardenias, with enormous crimson petals that glistened in the afternoon sun.

"I have something to tell you about these flowers," Isabel said.

She led us up the road by the house, then pointed to the hills off in the distance. "During the war," she said, "guerilla fighters hid in those hills and watched everyone who came and went. Many landowners were shot. But the guerillas knew how Doña María treated her workers, and they left her alone."

I wondered if this was just myth, a story inspired by a friend's loyalty. But Isabel took us up the road a bit farther, then stopped by a grove of trees. There, set into the grove, stood a small white chapel. Quiet and unassuming, it held the spirit of the sacred in its arched wooden doors, iron bell, and simple cross.

"Every Easter," Isabel said, "the workers make a heart of gardenia petals at the foot of the chapel doors. It's their way of thanking Doña María for her kindness."

I stared at the space before the wooden doors, picturing the Mayans in their embroidered blouses and white linen shirts, arranging a perfect heart of petals. Doña María represented everything the Mayan guerilla fighters rebelled against: colonial power, money, control. Yet she knew the name and history of every migrant worker on her property, even as thousands of workers in other parts of the country lay in unmarked graves. Taking the time to know those families was a simple thing, but it was acknowledgment, honoring the worth of each individual. *That's all anyone wants*, I thought. *That's why we fight all the battles in our lives.*

I could picture the gardenia petals lofting gently into the air and blowing away each Easter morning. Each of the hearts is a temporary tribute, yet its meaning is everlasting. Like other gardeners who work toward unity, Doña María created a space in which petals from a garden could form a flag of common ground. The path to peace is not complicated, she showed us. It's paved with simple respect.

gardener without borders

All of God's earth is holy ground.
—Joaquin Miller

In a small village in North Korea, greenhouses sit in view of majestic mountains with trees and crooked roads nearby. Sometimes wild pink azaleas bloom in the valleys well into the fall, and the unheated greenhouses nurture vegetables even in the bitter Korean winters.

Half a world away in North Carolina, three similar greenhouses sit in view of majestic mountains with trees and a path nearby. They are in an area known for pink azaleas. And they, too, shelter growing vegetables even in biting cold.

The greenhouses in Korea sit outside crude hospitals for tuberculosis patients; the ones in North Carolina outside a comfortable lakeside home. They are the results of efforts by the same man, a physician, who knows gardening and doctoring to be two forms of the same thing. I'm guessing he also suspects that healing the world doesn't have to be so hard. Maybe it can be helped with a few simple greenhouses.

His name is Dr. John Wilson, and I met him and his wife, Nancy, on an overcast June morning at their home in Black Mountain, North Carolina. We sat on their deck, where I soon discovered that their view of the world encompasses near and far like a high-powered telescope. Close up, you see hummingbird feeders and the bushy vine growing up the corner of the deck. Look out a bit farther where the yard slopes down to a lake, and you'll see three greenhouses and twenty community gardens, all under Dr. Wilson's direction.

Expand your view a bit more, and you'll take in all of Tomahawk Lake, which was an eroding mess until Dr. Wilson stepped in and helped shore up the banks and build gardens around it. Or you can tip your head back, relax, and look out in the distance over the water. There you'll see the point where two peaks of the Blue Ridge Mountains meet, making a V that looks like a migrating bird in flight.

Nancy, who will soon turn eighty-one, has just finished an hour of tennis with her friends on a court near the lake. Her white hair is short, styled in soft waves, and she moves with the sureness of a twenty-year-old.

Dr. Wilson just turned eighty-six the day before. Despite bypass surgery in 1992, he is robust and vigorous, with white hair and heavy white eyebrows that turn down over his eyes, making him look perpetually concerned, even when he smiles. He has been telling me about his gardens and travels around the world.

❦

The world in which Dr. Wilson grew up is one that most of us can't even imagine. Born in 1916 to U.S. missionaries in a southern province of Korea, he lived in an area of the country known, even in Korean terms of the time, for being backward. His parents had met in Korea; his father was a doctor and his mother a teacher, and they settled with their seven children in a twenty-acre missionary compound, creating an extended family.

In his early childhood, John attended a one-room school with other missionary children. He hunted deer and wild boar with his dad and four brothers, paid attention to his father's work with leprosy patients, and watched his mother earn the reputation as the best gardener in the compound.

After seventh grade, John attended boarding school and took his high school classes at the Pyongyang Foreign School (PYFS) in the northern part of Korea. The country was still united then. South and north were directions, not names. The trains ran the full six-hundred-mile length of the country in those days, so each fall, John climbed aboard a passenger car and rode for twenty-four hours to reach the school. He lived in a dormitory, studied with a girl named Ruth who would someday marry a man named Billy Graham, and played soccer with missionary kids who had been expelled from China by the Communists.

John Wilson and his brothers once predicted that they would grow up to be hunters and doctors like their father. For all of them, professions in health care followed, but somewhere along the way in John's life, hunting gave way to a maternal influence of gardening. Since his youth in Korea, he has remembered the days of unity, of trains that crossed no borders. He has used those memories partly as a physician, partly as a gardener, in both cases, to heal.

When the Wilsons moved to this home in 1975, the lake was unused, unappreciated, and effectively imploding, with soil washing down the unfortified banks and into the stagnant water. On its shore at the base of the Wilsons' property, several vagrants gathered each morning with cheap wine in brown paper bags. They sat under a cherry tree among overgrown weeds and vines, did their socializing, and left the bottles and bags behind. This did not go unnoticed by Dr. Wilson.

He wondered if the lake could be reclaimed, if it could become an attraction for families rather than transients. So he did some research, taking pictures of the lake, recording the erosion, developing ideas for reinforcing the banks and beautifying the area. He put together a plan and presented it to the city council. Before long, he found himself in charge of the reclamation project, choosing stone to line the eroding banks, erecting duck boxes and bird habitat in the middle of the water, and plotting out a lighted walking trail encircling the lake. The project grew into recreation areas with tennis and croquet courts. And now, next on the list, is a botanical/wildflower garden that Dr. Wilson and other gardeners are planting on the far side of the lake, in a spot the size of a football field that once was used as a dump.

"We went up to the Blue Ridge Parkway," he says, pointing to the top of the distant mountains, "to an area that's undisturbed." There were dogwood trees, he says, and ferns and lilies growing shoulder-high. The gardeners are transplanting some of those native species in the botanical garden. They'll also plant three hundred dollars' worth of wildflower seed, build walking paths, and erect signs in the spring, encouraging visitors to "pick a bouquet for your mother or grandmother."

The town is becoming a "flower city," says Dr. Wilson, and at the center of it is the once-neglected Tomahawk Lake, now known as the jewel of Black Mountain.

On this June morning, the view from the deck includes people jogging and walking around the lake. On the croquet course on the opposite shore, players dressed all in white look like tiny animated ghosts with sticks. At times, ducks land on the water, and clouds move across the mountains and disappear, constantly changing the view.

❧

The story of Dr. Wilson is not an easy one to tell. He has seen the country of his birth split in two. He has seen thousands of refugees pour into a camp where the medical care was administered by IVs slung from bamboo poles, and a mile-long trench served as a community latrine. He has seen the effects of female circumcision in Somalia, an imperial disregard for local people in Kenya, and the poverty that still exists in this country, even though we often pretend it doesn't.

Having completed his education in Korea, Dr. Wilson came to the United States and earned his degree in pediatric medicine. After he married Nancy, they moved to Greensboro, North Carolina, had six children, and put down roots. But, looking for new opportunities to serve, Dr. Wilson found work to be done elsewhere, some of it in his home country. The years between 1967 and 1977 read like a diplomat's dossier, with moves so frequent that the Wilsons' youngest daughter never attended the same school for more than two years in a row.

There were the years in South Korea where, accompanied by an evangelist and two nurses, Dr. Wilson drove an ambulance with coolers of polio vaccine into remote villages where the people had never seen a white person or a car. They screened the villagers for epilepsy, which had not been treated in Korea before, and then transported the sickest patients back to the city, where many were treated in the Presbyterian Medical Center where he worked as a missionary.

There were the years in Virginia, where Dr. Wilson treated rural residents of three counties. The people lived in shacks that had been granted to freed slaves after the Civil War. More than a century later, two-thirds of the shacks still had no plumbing or electricity, and the people were as short on fruits and vegetables as they were on jobs, heat, or medical care.

During the years in Kentucky, Dr. Wilson administered care to coal miners and their families through the Appalachian Regional Hospital. It was one of the most depressed areas of the country, he says, although residents had little garden patches on the mountainsides, where they grew crops of potatoes and turnip greens.

Even after the Wilsons moved to their current home in Black Mountain, Dr. Wilson was not to stay put for long. In 1976, he volunteered for several months at a refugee camp in Cambodia, where hundreds of refugees arrived daily, fleeing Pol Pot's murderous regime. The medical facility was comprised of several tents, sheltering patients who slept on mats on the ground. The patients lay in rows, and each morning the doctors started their rounds at the beginning of a row, moving from patient to patient on their knees.

Six years later, following trips to Kenya and Somalia, Dr. and Nancy Wilson volunteered for two months in Beirut after a massacre of Palestinians by the Lebanese "Christian Phalanges," assisted by the Israeli army. The first person Dr. Wilson saw when he went to the bombed-out first floor of the hospital was an eight-year-old boy who had been hit by shrapnel. He was sitting in a wheelchair, playing with a toy gun. This, however, was less shocking than what awaited Dr. Wilson in the obstetrics unit. There, the blood of babies murdered in the attack still stained the walls, as the Palestinians refused to wash it away.

He tells these stories with the composure of a man who has dealt repeatedly with suffering and war, but clearly, it confounds him that these events occur. Helping the world is like gardening, it seems. You can plant a seed and tend it, but there's another power that makes it grow

"God bless the U.S.A.?" Nancy says. "Forget it. God bless the world."

⁓

Not a person to sit still, Dr. Wilson jumps up and invites me on a tour of his gardens. He walks briskly, past a suspended metal pipe hung with containers of flowers, leading me toward the vegetable gardens. As we go, he stoops to examine the plants or rubs the top of his head, then points out an oriental persimmon tree, a rose of Sharon tree from Korea, apple trees, and blackberry bushes that yield by the bucketful.

He takes me to an area of hoop tunnels in which broccoli, kale, spinach, turnips, and brussels sprouts are growing. The hoop tunnels, like greenhouses in Slinky form, were inspired by a presentation he heard ten years ago at a North Carolina Organic Farming meeting on growing "cut-and-come-again" vegetables in unheated greenhouses. By building the greenhouses properly, the presenter claimed, you could grow vegetables in an unheated greenhouse even at temperatures of sixteen degrees below zero. Dr. Wilson decided he was on to something.

"When it's sixteen degrees below, you cover children with a blanket," Dr. Wilson says. "Same thing applies to plants." The blanket in this case is Reemay, a cheesecloth-like fabric made of spun polyester. With this system, he says, you can harvest winter broccoli, cauliflower, onions, and spinach, as well as lettuce that can be cut when it's two inches high, then regrown for continuous cuttings.

Down the hill from Dr. Wilson's gardens, the Black Mountain Community Gardens begin. It's hard to tell where one stops and the other starts; without dividing lines, they all blend together into one green space. But at the base of the Wilsons' property, where the drinkers used to sit, are twenty raised beds, offered to members of the community for twenty dollars each to grow their own vegetable gardens. For the past ten years, Dr. Wilson has assigned the garden plots, and he knows the people who tend them as well as the vegetables they grow. This one belongs to a librarian, this to a grandmother, that one to a university student, and that one to a woman with two children. "The gardeners fall into four categories," he says. "Good, Not So Good, Bad, and Not So Bad."

Nearby are gardens planted by two garden clubs for kids, which Dr. Wilson started. The children are from six to twelve years old, and they chose the names for their groups. The girls call themselves Gardeners of the Future, and the boys are Sprouting Seed. Dr. Wilson scratches the top of his head as he looks at the girls' bed, which he hopes will do better than last year. "I gave them an A for planting and an F for harvesting," he says.

One plot obviously belongs to a good gardener. "That man sifts his soil," Dr. Wilson says. The year before, one gardener grew pole beans on bamboo poles. "They grew up fifteen feet in the air," Dr. Wilson says. "He had to climb up a ladder to pick them."

Among the community gardens stand the three greenhouses that are visible from the deck. They measure ten by twenty feet and house head high tomato plants. One of them incorporates two tricks for generating and holding heat. The first is a sheet of red plastic that covers the floor. "It reflects the light, and the tomatoes ripen two weeks earlier," Dr. Wilson says. The second is composed of stones stacked along one interior wall. Dr. Wilson learned this lesson in radiant heat from a former doctor for the Atomic Energy Commission. The doctor mentioned to Dr. Wilson that the radiation of the atomic bomb in Hiroshima was still present in granite tombstones weeks after the blast. This piece of information might be lost on others, but for Dr. Wilson, it was transferable, just like the polio vaccine he carried in coolers throughout South Korea in the sixties. The idea—using stone to warm plants all winter—might have been rooted in conflict, but it could grow in peace.

❧

In the early 1990s, North Koreans were subsisting on a bit of grain, roots, and leaves. The United Nations predicted that, unless North Korea received massive aid, 20 percent of its population would starve to death the following winter. International help did come, but it was not enough. Ten percent of the population perished from starvation.

Measured against the predictions, you could interpret this as either a success or a failure. Dr. Wilson and others who had grown up in Korea viewed it as a situation that should never happen again. "That's when we started," he says.

We refers to alumni from Pyongyang Foreign School, those extended family members who shared space in the missionary compound long before Korea was divided. Now in their seventies and eighties, many of them were invited by a group known as Christian Friends of Korea, an organization for which Ruth Graham has served as honorary chairperson, to visit their homeland, where they began relief efforts of their own.

After an initial fact-finding trip, the alumni received a call from the North Korean ambassador in Washington, D.C., asking for another delegation to bring enough lettuce and spinach seed for a million farms. "They'd been very impressed with all these old people," Dr. Wilson says, "people who had been born there and spoke the language. They'd never seen such a concerned group."

In response to the ambassador's request, Dr. Wilson and his team shipped six hundred pounds of donated spinach seed and about one hundred pounds of lettuce seed. The following year, "everywhere we went, there was spinach growing," he says. "Even little hotels had their front yards plowed up and were growing spinach. We ate it three times a day."

With this success, it was time to think bigger thoughts. The alumni couldn't save the entire country, but they identified a particular need: the dozens of tuberculosis hospitals and rest homes throughout North Korea. A photo in a Christian Friends of Korea newsletter captures a TB rest home near the village of Anbyon. A long, low, primitive structure with few windows, it's set at the base of cone-shaped mountains, where it's fronted by a low stone wall, a few scraggly trees, and a winding dirt road.

Before the alumni's relief efforts, Dr. Wilson says, these types of dormitory-style facilities were understaffed and unheated. He knows from his youth that North Korean winters sometimes drop to thirty or forty degrees below zero and that food shortage is especially acute for hospital patients. Conditions were so poor that patients figured they were better off at home.

But when Dr. Wilson heard the explanation of cut-and-come-again vegetables, he knew he had an idea that might help the North Koreans. The greenhouses in his own backyard suddenly cut across borders, erased the vast space between the mountains of North Carolina and the mountains of North Korea, and became one of the centerpieces of the PYFS alumni's relief efforts. He built five more greenhouses, and he and his friends took them to Korea and set them up outside the hospitals and rest homes.

The logistics of transporting the greenhouses and other supplies are daunting, Dr. Wilson says. The team buys one or two twenty-by-eight-foot containers and fills them with greenhouse materials, supplies, and medicines. A truck takes them to Atlanta, then to San Diego, where they're shipped to China, a voyage of five weeks. The containers go through Chinese customs, then are loaded on a ship to Kimpo, North Korea, where they are sent on to Pyongyang by train.

It's equally difficult for the team to arrive. Many are elderly, and most have been missionaries or children of missionaries connected to Korea for much of their lives. The team flies to Seoul, South Korea, then to Beijing, China. In Beijing, they apply for a visa to enter North Korea. This is a time-consuming step. It's only a half-hour flight from Seoul to North Korea, but Americans can't fly across the demilitarized zone.

Over the past several years, the PYFS alumni have organized themselves and rallied, just like they did decades ago when they competed with the missionary kids from China on their school's soccer field. Their efforts have grown to such an extent that, in 2001, Christian Friends of Korea sent the following to North Korea: tuberculosis medicine for four thousand patients, soybeans, canned chicken, baby formula, microscopes, dentures, ambulance kits, four-wheel-drive vehicles, blankets, suction units, diesel generators, and an X-ray unit. They also took four thousand locust and cherry tree seedlings because the land has been deforested. And they took fifty large greenhouses.

By now, several hundred donated greenhouses, many of them twins to the ones in Dr. Wilson's backyard, dot the mountainous landscape of North Korea. A large number of them belong to the seventy-four tuberculosis hospitals and rest homes where, because of the fresh produce, medical supplies, blankets, and generators, patients now come to receive needed care.

When the PYFS alumni delegations visit North Korea four times a year, they're allowed to visit about a dozen of the hospitals, located in areas of the country that are considered less militarily sensitive. Some of those hospitals stand near the demilitarized zone, where the team sees the U.N. flag flying near fields of rice and barley. The North Koreans have built cement walls there, walls that can be blown up to close the highway in case of an invasion.

But that is half a world away.

The seedlings under the greenhouses in North Korea, in sight of military installations, are not that far removed from the tomatoes in the greenhouses here on the banks of peaceful Tomahawk Lake. Just like all the medications that Dr. Wilson has administered over his lifetime, the greenhouses in Korea are tangible. The community gardens are tangible. The new starts of eight foot high Turk's cap lilies, the Sprouting Seed, the lettuce that continues to grow for multiple harvests, they're all tangible. They are things that make sense, and they are things that can be controlled. The view from this deck can be close up or far away. It all depends on your perspective.

From the Wilsons' deck, you can see many things. You can see the life force that pushes a seedling out of the ground, the same force that will urge the human race forward as long as we don't stand in the way. And, with the help of Dr. Wilson's stories, you can see past that V in the mountains and understand what lies beyond.

The train still isn't running from North to South Korea as it was in John Wilson's boyhood. The flag still flies on the thirty-eighth parallel, marking the division line between his childhood home and his teenage school. It's just one of the world's many divisions, the deep lacerations that have left scars or have not even begun to heal.

A few weeks previous to this June morning, Dr. Wilson accepted the Peace Prize from Warren Wilson College in Asheville, North Carolina. It's an honor, to be sure. But for Dr. Wilson, the work is far from finished.

"Let me show you something," he says.

He goes into the house and brings a globe onto the deck. On it, little paper flags mark the spots where he and Nancy have lived and worked throughout their fifty-four-year marriage. Lengths of string in different colors connect the flags. Dr. Wilson has marked the globe this way to show his grandchildren, to keep a record of his life's work. The colorful strings are different, but in the end, they stretch in one continuous circle. Traversing boundaries, connected by oceans, they are all part of the same round sphere.

mother tongue

One touch of nature makes the whole world kin.
—*William Shakespeare*

Anna Wasescha observes and listens better than most people I know. She could probably be a great forensic scientist or a private detective, but she describes herself as the ideal liberal arts student instead. She's one of those people who takes twelve strands of thought from over here and a couple dozen from over there and a few thousand from all the places she's ever visited and everything she's ever read, then weaves them together into one huge web that creates something totally new.

This is how she created Farm in the City.

It started when Anna's son was little and she took him to Dunning Field near her house in St. Paul, Minnesota, to play ball. Each year, more than three hundred boys filled the team rosters for the Dunning Field games, and almost all of them were white, middle-class, and natively Minnesotan. There's nothing wrong with that, except that the makeup of those ballplayers didn't look anything like the neighborhood around them.

"The athletic lobby dominated the park," Anna says. Women were there to watch the boys play, and only a few girls ever came at all. In fact, while Anna's son spent plenty of time at the park, her daughter rarely had reason to go.

While the gender stratification didn't represent the neighborhood, neither did the split along cultural lines. The population around nearby Concordia University is racially, economically, and culturally diverse. Students and professors from other countries contribute to this mix. So does low-income housing.

Just two blocks east of Dunning Field, towering over this part of St. Paul just as the *Saturn V* rocket dominates the skyscape in Huntsville, Alabama, is the Skyline Towers, a twenty-one-story apartment building that houses what Anna calls "new Americans." They are recent immigrants and refugees from Sudan, Vietnam, Eritrea, and, in the largest numbers, Somalia. Uprooted from their own countries by war, political oppression, and unrest, they are fifteen hundred strong, and they are strait-jacketed in their building by language barriers and busy streets. It just happens that those two issues are strands in Anna's web of understanding.

❧

It's not unexpected that Anna would be drawn to international issues. Her husband teaches Asian history at a local college, and Anna holds a Ph.D. in educational policy. She's interested in the ways in which ideas from different disciplines merge, where they intersect and overlap, and how they can support one another. Her global perspective has been shaped by trips throughout Europe, Asia, and the United States, with her family often traveling garden to garden to observe the cultural and horticultural influences in each part of the world.

In 1992, Anna, her husband, and their three-year-old daughter spent three months living in Beijing, China, an experience that helped shape her view of the world. "The whole time we were there, I never saw a blue sky," she says. "The pollution was so bad, you couldn't even see across the street." People suffered chronic respiratory illnesses. They spat constantly, spreading infectious germs. "That's when I realized that breathing clean air should be a basic human right," she says.

She returned to the United States with a renewed appreciation of Minnesota and its blue sky. She came back with a new resolve, as well. "In my own corner of the world," she determined, "I can help the environment."

Those environmental concerns intersected with issues affecting the health and well-being of children, as well as the invisibility of immigrants in her neighborhood who, without the English language, had no voice. "I'm a well-educated white woman, and I appreciate how that's empowered me," she says. "I want to make sure it happens for other people."

So, in 1996, armed with her own belief system, a worldview, and skills in networking and advocating her mission, she set out to change her corner of the planet by starting a nonprofit organization called Farm in the City. At its heart is gardening, a universally accepted tool for self-expression.

Farm in the City has fostered a new level of social interaction and communication among neighbors in this older residential area of St. Paul. Elements of the organization spread out over an area of several blocks. At the center of its influence is Dunning Field, a park with ball diamonds, an administration building, and gardens planted as part of Farm in the City's youth and English-as-a-second-language (ESL) programs. Just north of Dunning Field is the campus of Concordia, where Farm in the City offers art classes to kids and has installed multiple gardens. The residents of Skyline Towers make use of the Farm in the City programs as well.

❧

Anna is relaxed and informal, yet she speaks with keen vision and clarity about the many facets of Farm in the City. She looks exactly like what she is: an educator, an environmentalist, and an activist. She is impassioned without being overly zealous, fervent while putting other people's needs first. Her graying brown hair is shoulder-length and parted to the side, and she is wearing sandals, shorts, and a white knit shirt on a muggy July day that threatens rain.

We have walked the three blocks south from Dunning Field to the Farm in the City Community Gardens, within view of the Skyline Towers all the way. Seventeen families from Skyline tend plots at the half-acre community gardens, but it's not easy for them to get here on foot. The apartments and the gardens are separated by an access road and a busy highway, which can serve as a barrier to people who don't yet feel safe in a new culture and environment.

"With your own street, you have a reasonable expectation that cars might be coming to your house or your neighbor's house," Anna says. "With the freeway and access road, you know that's just the public out there and they're not connected to you in any personal way. It's all very alienating."

The community gardens are flanked by old buildings; chain-link fences and power lines run along the back. Eventually the city will tear down the nearby buildings, and the land will be developed. But for now, Farm in the City has moved in, offering six-by-twelve-foot plots where the new Americans can grow the culturally distinct vegetables and herbs that will flavor their meals with reminders of home.

Anna and I are sitting on a picnic table with other representatives from Farm in the City. We're sitting on the table because tiny bugs, drawn by the garden beds around us, are biting our ankles. We're talking with Yi Yang, a Hmong man who came to the United States in the 1980s as a Laotian refugee. He is one of four deaf people from his Hmong hill tribe who are part of a pilot gardening program between Farm in the City and Mary Dykstra, a local woman who works with deaf refugees. Yi is telling us about gardening in Laos.

It's fascinating to watch this interview unfold. I ask a question of a hearing man who knows American Sign Language. In turn, he signs the question to a deaf woman who is bilingual: she knows American Sign Language and the gestural language of the deaf Hmong. She repeats the question in this language to Yi, who smiles at every query and happily signs his response. It takes four of us to ask and answer a single question. But this is fitting, the perfect symbol of a program that helps people communicate through the common language of gardening.

Yi is small in stature, with dark hair and glasses. Not

a resident of the neighborhood, he came to Farm in the City through his association with Mary. He rides his bike across town every day to spend two to three hours here weeding and working the soil, he says. At home he would be bored; here he is busy. He talks of the vegetables that he and the other three deaf Hmong gardeners have planted: tomatoes, green peppers, long red chili peppers, cucumbers, green beans, and super cayenne peppers. Those peppers elicit a broad smile.

Even though Yi and his fellow gardeners have broadened their produce beyond the rice and cabbage they grew in Laos, they are preserving some of their cultural heritage in this garden, Anna says, by planting labor-intensive mixed beds that are mounded to allow water to drain between the rows. This is how they would have done it back home, Yi says.

120   During the 1970s and 1980s, thousands of Hmong people were resettled in the Midwest, including the Twin Cities of Minneapolis and St. Paul. As a result, this small plot, tended by four deaf people from the other side of the world, makes these gardens more representative of the community at large.

As we leave to walk back to Dunning Field, we look for a moment at the entrance to the gardens, which has been decorated by a group of African-American youth engaged in an environmental program. Because this is a heavily trafficked street, both by cars and pedestrians, it's important for the gardens to enhance the appearance of the neighborhood, Anna says. But she bristles at the idea that all gardens are supposed to meet a homogenized U.S. standard. "We need to look at gardeners individually and let them garden in an individual style," she says.

The African-American teens have decorated the entrance their own way. They've sunk posts in the ground and painted them in bright blues and reds, decorating them with symbols and words like PEACE and RESPECT. On the ground, large painted stones spell out the word LIFE.

Back at Dunning Field, it's almost lunchtime for the kids and teens involved in another element of Farm in the City: the summer youth program. Close to fifty children are running around under the shade trees and climbing on the slides and swings. The ten adolescent leaders are looking like typical cool American teenagers, moving with a slow and practiced gait, seating themselves elbow to elbow with best friends around a purple picnic table painted with the words FARM IN THE CITY.

They're in the fifth week of the six-week summer program, which includes gardening, art, cooking, storytelling, drama, and cultural exchange. Because it's Latin American Week, the kids and teen leaders are studying the music, dress, food, and customs of the Hispanic culture. Some of the kids wear headbands they made out of orange paper, decorated with English words and sparkly stars. The teen leaders open their lunch bags and stretch out their legs around the table. Colorful playground equipment is within view, and the gardens are off to the side, occupying a corner of Dunning Field.

The teen leaders, ranging in age from thirteen to sixteen, come from Somalia, China, Ethiopia, and Minnesota. Several are here because they participated in the summer program when they were younger and wanted to come back as youth leaders. Ahmed, a thirteen-year-old from Somalia, was asked to be a teen leader by a woman who lives at Skyline. Bibi, fifteen years old and also from Somalia, has a brother and niece in the program; this way she can supervise them during the day. Molly, a fifteen-year-old from China, got involved because she played a native instrument for last year's Chinese Week and decided to come back as part of the staff.

This is not your typical summer job. The paid teen leaders are here every weekday from 8:30 A.M. to 3:30 P.M. And when they're not trying to keep the little ones from outsmarting them, they're directing art projects, cooking, and gardening.

The entire garden broadens the description of what's "American." Handmade signs designate the different flower and vegetable beds: THE CHILDREN'S GARDEN, SUN GARDEN, PIZZA GARDEN, and PRAIRIE RESTORATION. In the children's garden, a structure is made from a framework of rusted metal stakes, with vines climbing up over it and sunflowers growing inside. Some might liken it to a bean teepee, but here it's known as a bean temple, influenced by the same cultural diversity that placed a Hmong twig fence in the prairie restoration garden. The bean temple is distinguished by origami boxes and pieces of cloth that are tied to it, waving in the breeze.

Anna says that at the beginning of the garden season, in the Japanese Tanabata tradition, the kids wrote wishes on those strips of cloth and tied them to the temple. About 20 percent of the children are refugees or immigrants; the others have spent their lives, for the most part, in the Twin Cities. In either case, however, they probably have not been given much of a voice. Anna's out to remedy that. Give kids an opportunity, she says, and they'll tell you what they think. She quotes two of her favorite wishes from those tied onto the temple:

"I wish that I were not able to lie."

"I wish that all the magic in Harry Potter were true."

In gardening, you transplant seedlings when they're young and strong, able to slurp up large quantities of water, sun, and nutrients. Older plants don't like to be moved. They become susceptible to wilt and disease, like the pediatric syndrome "failure to thrive." They just can't adapt to their new surroundings, not when they're accustomed to a particular root system and climate.

The same can be said for immigrants and refugees. The kids pick up the language and the styles of dress and start hanging out with new friends; the parents stay in the relative safety of their new homes, lacking the language skills or energy needed to brave busy streets and red tape to break new ground. This is why Farm in the City incorporates a unique program, teaching Anna's new Americans a bit of the English language.

Marjorie Hundtoft has recently joined Farm in the City as the ESL coordinator. Like most of the Farm in the City staff and volunteers, her interests pivot around international issues and cultural exchange. Having lived in Africa during a study-abroad experience in college, she is now working with an ESL teacher to blend language classes with gardening for residents of Skyline Towers. Most of the residents come from equatorial Africa, but it's estimated that more than thirty languages are spoken at Skyline. The Farm in the City classes, offered through a partnership between the St. Paul public schools and

CommonBond's Advantage Center programming, help them break out of their microclusters.

One day a week, the adult students cross the pedestrian bridge over the congested freeway from Skyline Towers to Dunning Field, where Marjorie uses the forty-by-sixty-foot garden as a focal point for teaching English. Not only do the students pick up a few survival words like "hello" and "good-bye" and take part in some significant social interaction outside the long, unbroken corridors of Skyline, but they also can plant some herbs or vegetables in a communal setting. This is a critical factor among residents of Skyline; in the year 2001, 17 percent of them said they didn't have enough food to eat. This is, no doubt, a surprise to the immigrants; many of them came from places suffering from famine, expecting the American Dream to include food.

Anna remembers running into one of the students, Nyunget, at the grocery store. A native of Somalia, she still couldn't speak much English, but she hugged Anna and gave her a kiss and kept saying, "Garden, garden."

Marjorie starts each class by serving a dish prepared with vegetables from the Dunning Field garden. One day the students might cut into a beet cake; the next week they'll sample a salad. The recipes blend the students' cultural cuisines with produce available in the local markets. In addition, the foods serve as an automatic conversation starter for each class.

For some of the students, the Dunning Field garden is a training ground for new cultural norms and expectations. One instructor witnessed the tension among students who were accustomed to fighting for their territory in their home country. At first, they did the same in the garden, expecting that there wasn't enough room or food to go around. One of the students told the instructor, "We were fighting in our own country. Now we're fighting here. We don't need to do that." A cultural shift was taking place, as the immigrants accepted the Farm in the City garden as a place of security, of shared and common ground.

It's a testament to Anna's organizational skills and persistence that Farm in the City resides on both city property and on the campus of Concordia University, even though the program is not under the jurisdiction of either. Anna has amassed a team of volunteers, paid staff, funding sources, and teachers, as well as a board composed of businesspeople, educators, an attorney, an accountant, and a carpenter. The list of foundation and corporate support includes local businesses and arts organizations, as well as the Target, McNight, and National Science Foundations. This broad-based support has earned Anna the sanction of the university, which has itself opted to stay and expand in this diverse neighborhood rather than move to the suburbs.

On the grounds of the campus, Farm in the City has planted several gardens, including a labyrinth. Actually, it has planted two labyrinths. The first was dug up and moved to a new location to make room for a new college library. "When I found out they were putting the library there, I went through all of Elisabeth Kübler-Ross's stages of grieving in twenty-four hours," Anna says. But then the college told her the labyrinth wasn't being destroyed; it was simply being moved.

Anna shows me the new labyrinth, planted just two

months previously but thriving in a protected corner of campus. Near it is a sign cast from clay, bordered with painted imprints of ferns and leaves. LABYRINTH: AN AGE-OLD CEREMONIAL PATH OF RESTORATION, INSPIRATION, AND WISDOM, it reads. Labyrinths are known to be healing and meditative, as the walk to the center of the garden is symbolic of turning inward and becoming mindful of the messages from your own soul. In this labyrinth, based on three-thousand-year-old paintings from the Mediterranean island of Crete, the path is formed with plantings of widely diverse perennials, from wild roses and gangly daisies to low-growing dianthus and geraniums.

In the center are cement stepping-stones imbedded with broken shards of delft ceramics and mirror tiles, representative of everything from Minnesota's Dutch heritage to reflections of the soul. But also part of the labyrinth are special stones that came from an Indian tribal site in Minnesota, a spot considered sacred by the Native Americans. The site was cleared and paved for Highway 55, so Farm in the City moved the stones and gave them a place of honor in the labyrinth. Even here, in the silence of the meditative path, the disenfranchised have a voice.

When new Americans come to this country, they're often airlifted out of one world, in many cases out of one century, and set down in the middle of another. They are surrounded by the American Dream, but while that dream used to include a little house and yard to go with it, now it is more likely to be an apartment with no green space nearby.

The urge to garden is so strong that, in some places, immigrants will dig up a little strip of dirt next to a parking lot so they can raise a few vegetables or medicinal herbs. But at Skyline, there is no strip of dirt, nor any hospitable growing conditions. The wind that whips down the corridor created by the highway and the building is so strong, Anna says, that residents sometimes have to lean into it to walk along the side of the building and into their homes.

The soil on which we're raised holds memories and cultural beliefs, heritage, and ancestry. When you dig in the dirt, you touch things that are part of you, like the fragrance of the grass after your dad mowed the backyard, or the blackness of the dirt where you went hunting for worms on your uncle's farm. For some new Americans, they have to reach back further, before napalm, before famine, before a plane picked them up and brought them to a high-rise apartment building where a highway cinches them in.

This is why Farm in the City is like the heat under the melting pot, the energy that keeps it simmering and fluid. It recognizes that gardening is the most basic of languages, the labor from which we're all born and nourished. So now that Dunning Field looks like the community around it, it's time for the new Americans themselves to learn the next step of citizenship, letting their voices be heard. Anna considers it important to pass on the leadership of Farm in the City to young women and new immigrants. "I would consider it a failure if I were hit by a truck and that's the end of Farm in the City," she says.

It might not be the first generation of immigrants

who will take that step, but it will be their children, the teen leaders with their tie-dyed T-shirts and Somali head scarves, or the young women who brave the busy highway to plant herbs at Dunning Field. They are strands in the web of understanding.

"This is a stressed population," Anna says of the immigrants in the neighborhood. "We know instinctively that the green world feeds and clothes us. It also helps us heal faster."

So does giving voice to beliefs and desires, either in a new language or in the universal language of the garden. Through Farm in the City, the people in Anna's neighborhood have been listened to. These new Americans will move forward because they know it is safe to speak.

we the people

Pray for a good harvest, but continue to hoe.
—Old Saying

From the time immigrants flowed onto the eastern shore through the gates of Ellis Island, New York City has been the ultimate symbol of the national melting pot. It's the place where people of all cultures, races, nationalities, religions, and viewpoints converge on one small patch of ground, living together in such proximity that the democratic process is put to a minute-by-minute test.

Monuments like the Statue of Liberty and the evolving memorial at Ground Zero are immediately recognized as symbols of freedom. But throughout New York City, tucked around the corner from delicatessens or on the sunny side of high-rise office buildings, are less obvious symbols of democracy. They are the city's hundreds of community gardens. Like other outstanding features of New York, you may not see them until they stare you in the face. But if you saw them from the air, no doubt they would look like little oases, little places of green where people meet, lean on their hoes and spades, and talk about everything from their favorite mulch to their role in the democratic process.

Among all the community gardens in New York City, the Clinton Community Garden (CCG) may be considered the prime example. Like many of the others, it was started in the late 1970s, when the community garden movement began to take hold in New York. The city was a different place then. Many neighborhoods belonged to drug dealers, prostitutes, and street gangs. In a city close to bankruptcy, piles of rubbish lay uncollected. Upstart gardeners used to walk along the sidewalks, throwing tomato and wildflower seeds over the broken-down fences and into the vacant lots. If plants took hold and grew from the debris, then the gardeners figured other plants might, too. There they would stake their claim, like Gotham City pioneers.

In 1978, the land where the Clinton Community Garden now grows had been a desolate lot in Hell's Kitchen for close to thirty years. The 100-by-150-foot wasteland, sandwiched between two tenements, was covered with rubble, discarded appliances, junked cars, and at least one corpse since the lot had been used as a mob dumping ground. When a group of volunteers, led by Broadway dresser and painter Mallory Abramson, claimed the land for a garden, they secured the help of the sanitation department and the Medical Examiner in clearing the space. The junked cars, though, posed a bit of a problem.

Adam Honigman, one of the original volunteers, is known for working within the municipal system, giving it a slight nudge when it needs it. He recalls visiting the Sanitation Inspector to ask for help in removing the cars. When the Inspector claimed he didn't have the resources—

and Adam saw sanitation workers outside smoking by idle tow trucks—somehow the cars mysteriously ended up in the middle of 48th Street on a Wednesday afternoon, the matinee day for nearby Broadway theaters. The wrecks had mysteriously "levitated" out of the garden, thanks to some overnight help from a friendly private tow-truck driver. The inspector and his trucks hauled away the junked cars as the gardeners waved.

The garden has grown a bit since then. You could probably say that the democratic process has changed a bit, too, but one thing remains the same: These gardeners know how to get things done.

∽·

This is evident in talking with Annie Chadwick, the current chairperson of the Clinton Community Garden Steering Committee. We're sitting under the grape arbor on a sweltering day in July, when the thought of concrete streets and concrete buildings and concrete everywhere cranks up the internal thermometer another ten degrees. It's hot in the garden, but psychologically it's more comfortable than it would be out on the street. This is partly because of the cooling influence of the trees and grass and flowers. Partly, too, because of the sense of safety the garden provides.

The garden, accessible from 48th Street, serves the seventy thousand residents of Hell's Kitchen, which is bordered by 34th and 59th streets to the south and north, the Hudson River and 8th Avenue to the west and east. The neighborhood abuts Times Square, so if you venture just a few blocks, you're suddenly surrounded by marquees for *The Phantom of the Opera*, paintings on the exposed sides of seventeen-story buildings, and the place where the ball drops every New Year's Eve.

Hell's Kitchen has been greatly improved in the past five years. The rows of nineteenth-century red brick "railroad flats"—tenements with rooms lined up like railroad cars—were cleaned up and renovated. Vines grow up the wrought-iron gates in front of the buildings, and neighbors have planted flowers around the trees that grow out of narrow pits in the concrete sidewalks.

The neighborhood feels safe enough. Even so, the garden's seven-foot-high iron fence and locked gate provide an extra measure of security. Some city officials argue that this makes it inaccessible to the public, but the garden's governing board disagrees. Residents of Hell's Kitchen can get keys from the CCG Steering Committee, but if they don't have a key, they're not getting in. This means that there's no vandalism in the garden. It also means that once inside, you can stretch out on the grass and sunbathe, as a woman in a pink top and shorts is doing, or sit on a bench and read in the shade, as a studious-looking man is doing, without worry of being assaulted or mugged. It may be one of the only places in New York City where that's possible. You can meditate, stroll, dig, or weed, feeling like you're in a world removed from the city around you.

Having been repeatedly reelected, Annie is in her third year as chairperson of the steering committee, an organization of volunteers who now serve one- or two-year terms and oversee all the operations of the garden. Annie is an herbalist who, even when her term is up and she becomes what she calls a citizen gardener again, will still visit the garden twenty hours a week in the spring planting season, several hours a week for weeding in July, and a couple of times a week in the winter to forage for rose hips.

As we sit in the shade of the grapevines, Annie pushes her shoulder-length blonde hair back from her face and fills me in on the history of the Clinton Community Garden. Named for the preservation area in which it sits, it was laid out by the original volunteers. Their design, it turns out, has stood the test of time.

The volunteers designated the back one-third of the garden space for individual garden plots that now number 108. When the original gardeners dug up those spaces, they found spent bullets and old brick. Today, the four-by-eight-foot plots are something of a gallery, with bits of yard art and ornaments distinguishing each from the next. The gardeners who rent and tend these plots range in age from their twenties to their eighties, sharing tools stored in the CCG shed and swapping horticultural tips and summer-produce recipes.

The vegetable plots are fenced in with a separate gate, accessible only to those who tend them. This means that the more public area of the CCG occupies the front two-thirds, which was laid out, according to a gardeners' consensus, in walking paths and beds designated for different types of flowers and herbs. In the Native American garden, for example, grow Jacob's ladder, jack-in-the-pulpit, Virginia creeper, maidenhair fern, and other plants native to New York and New Jersey. The area also houses the garden's beehive, which is populated by thousands of Italian Caucasian honeybees. Each year, the gardeners harvest between eighty and one hundred pounds of Hell's

Kitchen Honey, which is sold during the neighborhood's Oktoberfest.

Nearby, a three-season bed adjacent to a towering Japanese magnolia is a shade-and-sun combination of hollyhocks, rudbeckia, and dahlias. All the beds are condensed, many underplanted, making the greatest possible use of the space. As in all of New York City, you stand in one spot and have one experience. You take two steps forward and have another.

The third and most critical thing the founding volunteers did from a design perspective was to plant green grass. Annie calls that lawn sacred. As we sit in the garden, I can see why.

A mother pushes her curly-haired daughter in a stroller. The mom is here to enjoy the flowers, but also because it's the only place around where her daughter can feel blades of grass between her toes; where she can let her daughter walk and fall down and crawl without worrying about cigarette butts or dog excrement; and where the girl will see birds and butterflies and maybe hear a bee. And if the girl wants, she can go to the two-by-three-foot corner of the garden where the soil is left unplanted so that kids can put their hands in the dirt and dig. If not for this, it's conceivable that hundreds and maybe thousands of kids in the neighborhood could grow to adulthood and never know the smell of soil.

These are all important experiences. But the lawn serves another purpose. It's a village green, the place where people who might never know each other can end up trowel to trowel, talking about what's going on in the school around the corner or the city offices down the street.

Over the past few years, there's been lots of talk among gardeners in New York City. And it hasn't all been in the gardens. Some of it has been in the form of debate at city council meetings. Some of it has taken place in interviews with reporters. Some of it has occurred when gardeners dressed themselves as flowers and vegetables and paraded down the streets of New York in a highly visible display of nonviolent protest. In each case, in fact, the gardeners were protesting a situation that threatened the community gardens of New York. As threats often do, the situation united the gardeners against a common enemy, and it planted the democratic process squarely at the feet of the people pulling rhubarb and mulching kale.

The problem started in 1998, when Mayor Rudolph Giuliani decided that the community gardens, which in many cases had catalyzed improvements in their neighborhoods, now were valuable pieces of property and should be returned to the city for development. He slated more than one hundred of them for auction, without entertaining suggestions about due process or alternate plans.

This did not sit well with the gardeners, whose collective sweat equity probably rivaled the construction of the Empire State Building. Because there are eleven thousand vacant lots in the city of New York, the gardeners didn't feel that the city needed their few hundred lots. Their anger wasn't just about the fact that they had worked hard in the gardens. It was a fear of losing something that had become so much a part of their lives. There's the benefit of fresh produce and the sensory satisfaction of flowers and bees. But on a much deeper level, the gardens are the place where the word *neighbor* is turned from a noun to a verb. Few parts of New York City offer a spot to sit still under a shade tree, meet the person from your building who lives three flights up, and have a conversation uninterrupted by honking cars or the pressure of the next appointment.

So when Giuliani made his pronouncement, the gardeners had something new to talk about in those shade-tree conversations. And they weren't talking tomatoes.

～

Adam Honigman says that community gardens operate as a microcosm of government. It's the best type of government, he says: People getting together and operating on a local basis, taking responsibility for cleaning up a lot, planting flowers, designing herb beds, and planning arts festivals and children's programs.

Because New York's community gardeners had already established these mini governments, they responded to the threat of extinction by doing what the democratic process is all about—organizing, attending meetings, making phone calls, and trying to convince elected officials that their voting block was large enough to swing an election.

In the meantime, the attorney general issued an injunction delaying the auction of the community gardens, and the Trust for Public Land, a national conservation nonprofit, stepped in and raised the money needed to buy sixty-two of the gardens if they ended up on the auction block. Adding her support, entertainer Bette Midler contributed seed money through her own foundation, New York Restoration Project, protecting the remaining fifty-one gardens from the auction block.

Through all of this, Annie Chadwick and Adam Honigman and the other volunteers and board members of the Clinton Community Garden worked with community gardeners throughout New York City to help build political capital. They were in a unique position; the CCG had been threatened with an auction of its own in the early 1980s, and the gardeners had started a Square Inch Campaign, "selling" square inches of the garden for a five-dollar donation to raise money for outright purchase of the land. After nationwide attention, the auction was postponed, and the CCG was transferred from the Housing Preservation and Development Department to Parks and Recreation. This made the garden the first in New York City to receive the permanent protection of parkland status. In 1998, then, the CCG was not in jeopardy from Giuliani's decision. But instead of sitting back and observing the court battle from their protected status, the Clinton Community Gardeners helped lead the fight to save all the endangered gardens in New York.

The reason for such solidarity, Annie says, is that the situation is one all community gardeners face, and not just in New York City. Throughout the country, community gardens may be threatened with similar unilateral decisions as land for development becomes more valuable. What city leaders often don't consider, she says, is that land values go up *because* the gardens exist; reclaiming the land for development could be more expensive than city leaders think. In Hell's Kitchen, real estate brokers make annual donations to the CCG because they know it ups the neighborhood's land values and, thus, their commissions. Throughout the city, apartments that overlook gardens are sold or rented for more money than those without a garden view. And if Adam Honigman had to guess how much the Midtown Manhattan land is worth on which the CCG is sitting, he'd estimate it at between five and ten million dollars.

The financial figures are convincing, but money is not what the gardeners are afraid of losing. Many of them wouldn't have a green space if it weren't for the gardens—no place to get away, no place to go on a long weekend. "For many people," Annie says, "this is their Hamptons."

In many ways, gardens offer a slice of life that wouldn't be available otherwise. One gardener in another part of Manhattan, for instance, says that her garden's steering committee once had a discussion about planting cherry trees in the garden. They voted to plant them, partly for this reason: Where else in the city would kids get the experience of swiping cherries from a tree?

Each of the community gardens in New York operates a little differently. Some are gated like the Clinton Community Garden and others are unfenced and rely on regular patronage to keep vandalism down. Some divide public space and private plots according to a different ratio. But in the end, they all provide one key characteristic to their neighborhood: A public meeting place where neighborhood events can be held.

At the Clinton Community Garden, the steering committee has started offering July 4th barbecues in the park so that neighbors can take part in an essentially American activity. In the spring, local residents come to bless seeds in an annual ritual, and in the summer they participate in a solstice ceremony. People can also rent the space for weddings and family events. As with other gardens around the city, this green space was also the place where people came after September 11 to heal. They could walk to the Clinton Community Garden, unlock the big iron gate, let themselves in among the fall dahlias and green grass, appeal to the sky, and try to make sense out of a world raining down on them in clouds of debris and ash.

✑

On September 26, 2001, just over two weeks after the World Trade Center attacks, a benefit concert was held at the Clinton Community Garden. The purpose was twofold: to raise money for the families of the thirty-eight Hell's Kitchen firemen who died in the attacks, and to give neighbors a chance to congregate in their grief.

The gate was wide open, and five hundred people crammed themselves into the garden and spilled out into the street. When the firemen arrived, driving up 48th Street in their trucks, it was as if the sea parted, Annie says. "They got down off the trucks and shook everybody's hand."

That evening, the garden raised several thousand dollars, mostly in singles. Soon, with the help of a few more garden friends from out of town, the CCG steering committee presented the families of the lost firemen with a total of six thousand dollars, some jars of honey from the CCG beehives, and keys to the garden—an invitation to come and find peace. The event was considered so significant that the steering committee voted to hold an annual Hell's Kitchen picnic to honor local firefighters and police, to be held on the fall equinox.

If it hadn't been for the garden, Annie adds, "where would this have been possible?"

On a summer's day, Adam Honigman is carrying an umbrella, swinging it back and forth Gene Kelly style as we walk the Hell's Kitchen neighborhood. Using his umbrella as a pointer, he indicates every garden space tucked away between buildings. He also knows every building that's due to be torn down, what's going to take its place, and how the Hudson River green space has affected the neighborhood. He knows, as others do, that the park just down the street from the CCG still has problems with drug dealers, and that volunteers who planted some flowers there saw them ripped up within two weeks by vandals. Most important, he knows that the way to keep making progress in the garden is to be aware of what's going on in the city.

But the act of gardening itself does not get lost in the politicking. Adam is the one who takes the subway down to Union Square to buy new flower plants at the market, rehabilitating the beds in the CCG if they start to fade in the city heat.

Some of Adam's approaches may be unconventional, but he has a deep understanding of the intersection between the Clinton Community Garden and the democratic process. "Do we have parties honoring the parks commissioners and elected officals?" he asks. "Of course we do." Work within the system, he says. "It's the most American thing to participate in your neighborhood and the political process."

Within the CCG, this means setting up a governing board, following through on problem solving, dealing with a budget, and providing safety and security in the garden. In the larger community, it means attending city council meetings, calling the aides of elected officials, and taking an active interest in the future of the city.

In response to such efforts by community gardeners throughout the city, the Attorney General of New York issued a statement in September 2002, saying that a resolution had been reached in the lawsuit over the development of property containing community gardens. According to the statement, the city agreed to offer 198 sites to the Parks Department and/or to not-for-profit land trust organizations for preservation as community gardens or open space. The city also agreed to offer protection to 197 gardens that are already preserved and to not develop 100 gardens maintained by the Department of Education. In addition, the agreement establishes a review process for gardens slated for development and a license for residents to operate community gardens

This is at least a partial victory for the gardeners; it preserves hundreds of existing gardens, but it does not include a process for creating new ones. Still, it's proof that people who plant can also be people who plan, implement, strategize, speak, and persuade.

The democratic system may grow from deep roots, but it bends to meet the needs of the people. As the community gardeners remind us, we are all standing on the same soil. The garden flourishes when everyone helps to hoe.

gardens that inspire

I have tried being a successful container gardener. I really have. Every spring I go to the nursery and buy hanging baskets of fire-engine-red geraniums, pink Waverunner petunias, and purple impatiens so thick they look like a helmet of blossoms. This year I bought a particularly spectacular hanging basket planted with three frilly kinds of flowers: salmon-colored verbena, lavender nemesia, and yellow osteospermum, which to me look like little butter-yellow daisies with deep purple centers. Within weeks— actually, within days—they were looking parched, then droopy. Then dead.

To tell the truth, the best luck I've ever had growing plants on my patio was the year some dirt collected in the crease of the cushions on my deck chairs, and yarrow seeds from a nearby bed took root and sprouted.

I do not call this success.

It's a little embarrassing, really. Especially when you find out about somebody like Julia Nahring. Julia lives in Kalispell, Montana, just sixty miles from the Canadian border, which means that her growing season lasts about two-and-a-half weeks. This year, after a cold and wet spring, Julia planted her container garden by mid-June, but by mid-August, she was covering the vegetables to protect them from early frosts.

What's remarkable about Julia—aside from the fact that she has a twenty-by-forty-four-foot deck, the deck is filled with container plants, and the plants all look like someone went wild with a new set of tempera paints—is that she's eighty-two years old and in a wheelchair. She had polio back in 1951, and after eighteen years of raising her three children while she was on crutches, she conceded that it might be nice to sit down. Now she has two electric wheelchairs so she won't waste any time; she zips around the house and deck in one chair while the battery on the idle chair recharges.

Julia was a California girl for sixty years but moved north to be near two of her grown children. She ended up building a home right next door to her daughter and son-in-law, where her deck overlooks a river, a wooded island populated by deer and blue heron, pine trees that go on for eternity, and wildlife of every description. "I looked out one day and there was a moose plodding along the riverbank like an old donkey," she says. He went uptown, cut through a bunch of yards and scared people to death, then turned toward the river and went on his way.

She decided that if she was going to be a Montanan, the only proper thing to do was to act like a pioneer woman, so she equipped her house with a wood-burning stove, and every fall when the first snow came, she "jumped up and down in her wheelchair," she says.

Clearly, Julia doesn't pay much attention to what some would call a disability. To get things done around the house, she makes do with what she has. If she needs to pull clothes out of the washing machine, she uses a wooden spoon. If she needs to move canisters to the edge of the kitchen counter, she enlists the help of a long-handled fork.

Out on the deck, she could make use of all sorts of new garden tools that manufacturers have designed for people with everything from arthritis to blindness: light-weight hand tools, raised beds on tall legs that put flowers and vegetables at wheelchair height, pulleys that lower hanging baskets for deadheading, and planters on wheels, just to name a few.

But Julia only makes a couple of concessions in her garden. She does use a lightweight trowel and fork. And she enlists the help of her fourteen-year-old grandson to lift bags of potting soil and fertilizer in the spring. Other than that, she's pretty self-sufficient. "If I need to move a rose planter around," she says, "I just put my wheelchair in gear and bulldoze it."

Julia varies her selection of plants from year to year, spending her winters poring over garden catalogues and choosing a theme for the coming growing season. A few years ago, it was miniatures. "Baby eggplant, the tiny ones. Four or five kinds of tiny squash, baby carrots, baby everything," she says. She had a good time calling nurseries all over the country to see what they had.

"I just do it for fun," she says. "I have corn waving around, and green beans. I pulled peas out last night. I have tomatoes and peppers and all kinds of herbs. Just the things a guy would like to eat." Or a rugged Montana kind of gal like Julia.

This year, she's also growing delphiniums, black-eyed Susans, sunflowers, petunias, and Jubilee marigolds that will hold their color until late in the fall. She's set frog and squirrel yard ornaments around, maybe to keep the raccoons company when they raid the place at night.

Julia goes to bed at sundown most nights because she's tired out by then. Napping doesn't work so well because by the time she takes off the leg braces, gets into bed, and puts them back on after her rest, she might just as well not have rested at all. But she's not complaining. She's got more productive activities waiting for her out on the deck.

When you're focused on a plant, I guess you're less likely to think about what hurts, who hurt you, or why you think you can't do something you really can. Like grow healthy plants in Wal-Mart chair cushions.

Some people see roadblocks and stop. Others see roadblocks as detours and find another way.

"I'm very fortunate," Julia says. "Always have been."

market day

All work is as seed sown; it grows and spreads,
and sows itself anew.
—Thomas Carlyle

Trudi Temple holds a butterfly net in one hand and a pair of pruning shears in the other. She is ready to use them both. Trudi is not the Wyatt Earp of the garden, but she *is* determined. Secondary buds on peonies don't belong in her garden. Nor does she tolerate the small white butterflies that infiltrate her yard. As soon as one of those butterflies comes into view, she's after it, swooping the net over her head and bringing it to the ground, where she squishes it with her heel. This morning, she has done away with three of them, effectively eliminating the hundreds of worms they would have produced. This year, they will not infest her broccoli. "If they have some little bit of a brain," she says, "they'll fly far away."

149

Trudi's determination is a major part of her DNA; it's as evident as her German accent and the hole in the knee of her sweatpants. "I believe in using things up," she says.

Determination is the thing that turned her home's ample yard into the equivalent of a botanical garden. Her house, a European-looking half-timbered structure, sits outside of Chicago. Out front is a tall wrought-iron fence, and inside the gate is the first of many beds of flowers. The front is pretty enough, with pine trees along the driveway and tulips in the front bed. But walk around to the backyard, and you'll be looking around for an admission booth.

Serpentine beds ablaze with color wind through the immaculate yard. The beds contain masterfully arranged plants of every description, some grown for their foliage, others for color and bloom. Trees are planted in harmony with the flowers and shrubs; in the early May morning sun, the blooms of the newly opened redbuds glitter like pink pearls. Across the yard, a graceful iron arch that Trudi designed creates visual division and structure. Another arch, nearer the house, holds several bells from different parts of the country; Trudi intends to fill the arch with an entire collection that will ring out with the wind.

Every one of the thousands of plants has received its due attention. A sequoia tree that Trudi bought in 1970 for twelve dollars now stretches so far to the sky that you have to tilt your head back to see it. A cypress tree that she bought for five dollars sits like a sculpture, having been pruned like a delicate flower. "I like to take all the bottom branches off the trees," Trudi says. That's why a deep-purple lilac that took Trudi years to find is trimmed like a dainty parasol.

Trudi's hair is caught up in a bun; her face is bright and unreserved, and her voice trills up and down when she talks. Although she's always in action, she carries herself with a sense of freedom and lightness, as though she cares deeply about a lot of things in life, but taking herself seriously is not one of them.

Under a shade tree sits a bed frame made out of logs. In the place where the mattress would be, she has filled it with rich soil and planted white impatiens, making a true flower "bed." Even her woodpile adds to the design of the garden. It's stacked out behind the house, off the kitchen. "I don't burn the wood," she says. "I just like the way it looks. The texture is nice, don't you think?"

Despite the grandiosity of her gardens, though, they're not really what her story is all about. They could be; in fact they've been featured in several garden magazines, with photographs of the waterfall and holding pools lined with Wisconsin stone, the handmade benches that overlook beds of perfectly harmonized foliage and flowers. It is a photographer's dream, Trudi's garden, and a place that makes the phrase "stop in your tracks" real. You have to. It's that beautiful.

But that's not what Trudi's story is all about.

Her story is about what she calls stubbornness, and what anyone else would call clear-sighted vision that should be bottled and given away free to politicians. It turned her yard into a private park.

It also turned a simple fund-raising idea into a life-changing operation.

∽

Trudi grew up, prophetically enough, in a German town called Blumenau, or "flower meadow." Married young, she soon divorced. Her father advised her to go out and meet people, but she had determined that marriage was not for her. Life, however, had other plans. It was the early 1960s. She was dusting one day, and her future was about to arrive.

"In Germany," Trudi says, "when you do the house-cleaning, you dust with a rag, and then you shake the rag out the window." After one good shake, Trudi looked down from the second-story window and saw that she had just sprinkled dust on a couple of young men walking past. As it turned out, she knew one of them, and after talking through the window for a few minutes, she decided she had no choice. "I invited them in for a Coke."

Before long, she found herself attracted to her acquaintance's friend. His name was William, he was from Brooklyn, New York, and he was an army aviator. This was their first meeting, but not their last. In 1963, Trudi immigrated to the United States, met up with Bill again, and they married. Eventually they moved to a suburb of Chicago, and Trudi found herself in charge of a large house with the pitched roofs and half-timber construction of the houses back in Germany. "We didn't have money to decorate the inside," Trudi says, "so I decorated the outside."

Having grown up in a place like Flower Meadow, Trudi had been privy to the achievements of some of the world's best everyday gardeners. "I thought marrying and gardening went together," she says. "I didn't know you could be married and *not* garden." And so she started in, a young bride equipped with memories of European gardens and an endless supply of fortitude.

❧

Trudi gardened between trips around the world, made possible by Bill's career. In the South China Sea, she witnessed impoverished families turn *sampans*, or junks, into overcrowded houseboats. "When a hurricane comes up, whole families get lost," she says. "I was taken by that and tried to help them have dwellings. It opened up my eyes to the needs of people in other parts of the world."

With her husband, a humanitarian in his own right, she witnessed poverty in Borneo and Hong Kong. Before long, Trudi was opening her wallet whenever she could.

"I developed an eye for missionary families," she says. She could spot them a mile away. Once, while standing in line at the airport, she wondered why the line wasn't moving. When she stepped up to see what was going on, she saw a family with several children. "Missionaries," she said. On their way to Africa, they had too much baggage and no money for shipping. Trudi asked them how much they needed and wrote out a check.

Now, decades later, she is out front of her house, near the six-foot-high wrought-iron gate. She sees no butterflies, but she spots a jogger going by. "Good morning," she calls out, so it's almost like singing. "Happy springtime."

The jogger doesn't look up, but Trudi doesn't mind. "I like the excitement of making people happy," she says. "It's been important for my own enrichment, or what I've done wouldn't have worked."

❧

During her years of travel, Trudi kept gardening and developed quite a plant collection. In 1973, she had just returned from Hong Kong where again, she had seen refugees from China living in impoverished conditions. A pastor had told her that seven hundred dollars would pay for a house for a family, but she didn't have seven hundred dollars and wasn't sure where to get it.

Back home in her garden, she realized she had the help she needed in her own yard. She started making and selling flower arrangements for weddings and parties, and she sold plants that she started and nurtured. In the winter, though, she had nothing to peddle. So she took the next step, heading to the Randolph Street Market in Chicago, forty-five minutes away, to buy her cold-weather flower stock. She awoke at one o'clock in the morning to make the trip, entering a world of trailer trucks, loading docks, and truckers who threw around words Trudi hadn't heard when she was learning to speak English.

Before the winter was over, she discovered that the market sold more than flowers; it had vegetables, too. So taken was she with the fresh oranges and cauliflower that she bought thirteen cases of fresh produce and lugged it all home. Bill took one look at it and reminded Trudi of one simple fact: The two of them, plus their two small daughters, couldn't eat thirteen cases of vegetables. "Find somebody to share it with," Bill said. So she did. Trudi offered it to their friends at a ten percent markup, and the profit went to mission work. The friends loved it, the ten percent started adding up, and Trudi's fund-raising co-op was born.

Pretty soon, the co-op was growing, always by the dozen, Trudi says. "Twelve people were perfect for sharing a box, because there would be seventy-two oranges, twelve cauliflower, twelve heads of lettuce." Trudi needed a truck to bring it all home. Within a year, she was sharing it with eighty-four families, making those one A.M. trips once a week.

One day, in 1975, Trudi's daughter Trudianne, a second-grader at the time, came home from school and said she needed a cake to sell for a school fund-raiser.

"I don't want to bake a cake that will sell for half of what it's worth," Trudi had said, and she offered to give her ten dollars instead.

Upset, Trudianne couldn't wait for her father to come home so she could tell him what a mean mother she had. "He agreed with her," Trudi says, "and he made it absolutely clear that I could not send her to school with ten dollars when everyone else would be bringing a cake." Bill challenged Trudi to think of a better option.

That's when Trudi thought of her co-op idea. Why not apply it to school fund-raising? They could have a market day at school, selling produce for the same ten percent markup Trudi offered to her friends. It was a hit. Trudi set out the food in the school gym, and the project raised more than three hundred dollars. Pretty soon the principal called and said parents were asking to do it again.

Once a month, Trudi set up shop in the school gym, and the proceeds went back into the school for special programs. Then other schools heard about it, and churches heard about it, and Trudi expanded her efforts. She called the project Market Day, officially naming the nation's first food co-op school fund-raiser.

Trudi continued to get up at one A.M. and drive several times a week to Chicago, where she bartered with the produce salesmen, persuaded them to clean up their language, and carted the food home for sale. As soon as she got home, she set the table for the evening meal. "I had no idea what I would make for dinner," she says, "but it built a good attitude." It was a clear intention, an expectation that dinner would be created, and it always was.

After years of early mornings and unplanned meals, Trudi answered her front door one evening to find a man she didn't know standing on her front stoop. His name was Greg Butler. A local government employee, he had heard about Trudi's operation and wanted to know more. One morning he accompanied her to Chicago, and when they returned home, he looked at Trudi and said, "Lady, you work too hard." A couple weeks later, he called back to ask how he could help. "He suggested that if I taught him my methods," Trudi says, "he could drive to Chicago one night a week so I would have one good night's rest."

So every Wednesday, accepting no money for his efforts, Greg made the early morning rounds to the Randolph Street Market. Two years later, he quit his day job and joined Trudi in forming Market Day Corporation.

Since then, the corporation has hired a staff of fifteen hundred people, added services like FTD floral delivery, rented warehouses and built one of its own, bought a fleet of trucks, and produced a Web site that offers far more than fresh produce. Featured foods might include chicken tenders, beef stroganoff, or lemon pie. If you're a harried parent who needs a quick dinner menu, the Web site provides that, too, complete with recipes using some Market Day products as ingredients.

The project has spread to thousands of schools in the Midwest and east coast, with parent volunteers taking orders and coordinating pickup of the delivered goods. The schools are guaranteed a ten percent profit, but the proceeds sometimes exceed that figure, climbing as high as thirty-five percent. In Wisconsin, five hundred schools participate; together, they average about two hundred thousand dollars in profits each month.

That kind of money makes almost anything possible. For a school in Cape Girardeau, Missouri, for instance, the money will make it possible to open a new media center and library. Other schools have purchased computers, books, playground equipment—even buses.

All told, the money schools have made from Trudi's Market Day in the past twenty-seven years approaches three hundred million dollars.

That's three hundred *million* dollars. And it all started with a garden.

Not everything blooms under Trudi's direction. A few years ago, she turned her considerable efforts toward a small village in New York, where her husband's family owns a cottage. Trudi was always struck with how forlorn the village looked. "I would marvel at what was not happening there," she says. "People sat in molasses."

Being Trudi, she had an idea: Plant daylilies everywhere. Make this the daylily capital of upstate New York. Plant so many daylilies that people from all over would be drawn to the village to see them. Businesses would boom, the town would earn its mark on the map, and the little village would blossom into its full potential.

A few people were excited by the idea; the rest were suspicious. But when Trudi donated ten thousand daylilies, the plan started to work. Homeowners transformed their postage-stamp lawns into gardens, and local TV crews came by. Motorists slowed down on their way through town, and the houses scattered throughout the village started to emerge from molasses. But the pull of the status quo was too strong.

After a while, townspeople stopped weeding, and they never made an attempt to merchandise the flowers. Then they started ripping out the daylilies and planting petunias.

Discouraged and disappointed, Trudi abandoned her idea. Some people would have grumbled. Some people never would have gone back. But Trudi just stopped speaking of daylilies and turned her attention elsewhere. She's not one to get stuck in molasses herself.

Trudi still lives in that European-looking house that was once empty of furniture. Before we go inside, she takes off her garden clogs and puts them in an old weathered cupboard on the front stoop. There's a bench, a broom for sweeping the stoop, and birdhouses everywhere. A sign nearby reads HAUS BLUMENAU.

Inside, a huge dining room table is covered with a patchwork quilt. On it is a shovel filled with yellow apples. "My trademark," Trudi says. She goes into the kitchen, opens the refrigerator, and pulls out shrimp and cocktail sauce and a soup made with vegetables and Russian tarragon from her garden.

Pretty soon we're sitting at the long pine kitchen table, and I'm admiring the teapot collection on the wide ledge behind the sink and the soft green of the paint-washed cupboards. Trudi has been telling me about the neighbor at her farm, which is located near Rockford, Illinois. One day a couple of years ago, before she knew him well, he was walking past her farmhouse and she noticed he looked dejected. "You look like you have a heavy heart," she said to him. He sat down in the grass and started talking. "We've been talking ever since," she says.

This is the way things go with Trudi, I imagine. She will do anything she can to help you. "I learned early on that it's better to receive a smile than a frown," she says.

The phone rings and she talks with her sing-song German voice, like the call of a bird. She peels kiwi while she talks and sets a plate in front of me. I'm trying not to slurp my soup because she has just commented on her farm neighbor's nice eating habits. She pays attention to these things, just like she pays attention to the many shades of hosta in her garden and the way two pear trees grow toward each other to form an arch over the drive. The phone rests on her shoulder while she talks and peels. "I try to make good use of all my minutes," she says.

This efficiency clearly is one of the keys to the accomplishments in her life. As we finish lunch, I ask her what else she considers her guiding principles. Obviously, she doesn't much like swearing, or she wouldn't have broken the truckers of it. And she is allergic to chaos, she says. But there are other rules of thumb: Don't feel sorry for yourself. Be wise with your money. Drink lots of water. And don't stress out if something doesn't get done. "I know as I look back I did the best I could every day," she says.

The most important principle of all, though, is very simple, Trudi says. "Don't expect anything." She tells her kids not to buy gifts for her birthday, and she doesn't know when Mother's Day is. "They don't need the pressure," she says. Free of expectations, she is also free to be completely delighted when a thoughtful act or comment crosses her path.

❧

Who knows what Trudi will create next? At this stage of life, she is content to be in her own garden, chasing butterflies and potting up plants for gifts. At the back of her yard, a large area is fenced in all around and overhead to keep out marauding critters. This is where Trudi raises vegetables and starts her garden plants. It is, in effect, her own private nursery. Whenever she thins out plants in the yard, she digs them up, sets them in a one-gallon black plastic pot with a helping of her rich compost, and waits for the day when she will need that bleeding heart in a different part of the yard, or she's going to a friend's house and wants to take a primrose along.

She also has a plan for her flower gardens: tagging every plant, then making a visitor's guide so that guests can wander around and admire her yard for the botanical garden that it is.

But Trudi has other ways of making use of her minutes. She's already thinking about fall, when she and her daughter Margo will hold another of their autumn festivals at Trudi's seventy-six-acre farm. Scheduled for the third weekend in October, it will feature three days of live music (including bagpiping by Margo and her husband, Adrian), wagon and pony rides, local craftspeople, refreshments, a bonfire down in the meadow, and a barn decorated with dried flowers and between sixty and one hundred of Trudi's floral arrangements, made from flowers she's dried all summer long.

Trudi and Margo plan and organize the entire weekend, and all the help is voluntary. It makes Trudi so tired that she's "walking on her knees" by the end, but it's fun, she says, as the trill in her voice heads skyward.

This may look like a charmed life. How else could a girl from a small village in Germany end up in an affluent Chicago suburb and go on to raise millions of dollars for people around the country? But Trudi is like a living, breathing, butterfly-chasing example of the fact that fulfilled desires are not a bad thing. If we have what we need, then we can focus our attention on those who have greater needs than we do. People who believe right along with her have bought essential equipment for their schools. Those who don't have seen the daylilies in their front lawns wither away and die.

Market Day is still going strong, serving more than six thousand schools in twenty-one states. In addition to the in-school orders, it has filled almost five million orders online, with customers designating the school to which profits should be credited. Still, times are getting tougher, Trudi says. For one thing, many more women work outside the home now than they used to, making it more difficult to arrange the pickup of the food. But as long as the venture keeps breaking even, Trudi says, she'll keep it going.

Three hundred *million* dollars.

That's a lot of determination. The white butterflies don't stand a chance.

fresh start

Seeds of discouragement will not grow in a thankful heart.
—Anonymous

Jessica Prough's world is a bit small right now. It consists mainly of a three-square-block area in Toledo, Iowa, population 2,451, a town whose slogan is "Remembering Our Past. Looking Toward the Future." Toledo's biggest employer is a Pioneer Hybrid Corn production plant; the town has six insurance agents, three taverns, three agricultural supply dealers, two auto body repair shops, three churches, and nine barbers and beauty salons, including Beauty Cove and Kountry Kutter. The town is the seat of Tama County, and people stay in its four motels and eat at the Fireside Black Angus Bar and Grill partly because it sits down the road from the Meskwakie Indian casino, a structure that sticks out of the rural landscape for the simple reason that it was built to look like a feathered headdress. Jessica sometimes helps usher at the casino concerts; otherwise, entertainers aren't much a part of her world. The three-block area in which she lives is the Iowa Juvenile Home.

When I drove into town and stopped to ask directions to the Juvenile Home, the woman behind the Kwik

Star counter looked for just a moment like I'd uncovered a family secret, and she was sizing me up. Was I the mom of a kid gone wrong? A state worker on assignment? Worse, a reporter?

"Turn left at the blue motel," she said.

A couple blocks down the street, I came to Jessica's world.

The Iowa Juvenile Home is not a bad-looking place. In fact, the 1920s buildings, formerly used as a college and an orphanage, have been smartly remodeled. The biggest structure on campus is the academic building, which is where I met Jessica.

At eighteen years old, she stands just over five feet tall. You'd probably peg her for a fourteen-year-old, especially when she smiles, because somehow her freckles are more noticeable then. Shoulder-length blonde hair frames her face, she has the tomboyish build of a softball player, and she wears a green polo shirt and jeans, the uniform of the Juvenile Home. Her real home is just ninety miles away in the southern-Iowa town of Chariton, another county seat with a population of forty-six hundred.

Jessica has lived at the Juvenile Home for the past seven months, and she'll be here one month longer. On an August afternoon, I'm sitting next to her in the vocational classroom, which is a jumble of signs, books, videos, and bright yellow plastic storage containers labeled with the names of various vocational projects. Desks and chairs are haphazardly arranged. One table holds a window fan and about three-dozen fresh tomatoes spread on a green tablecloth. Jessica is showing me a PowerPoint presentation, replicating the one she and two other girls gave at a vocational SkillsUSA-VICA (Vocational Industrial Clubs of America) competition in Kansas City, Missouri, two months earlier. She starts the presentation by saying, "I'm Jessica Prough. I was a user and a dealer. I'm a person in need."

The presentation chronicles the girls' efforts to grow a garden and donate the food to the Tama County, Iowa, Food Bank. This was a stretch for Jessica. Since getting heavily involved with drugs, she lost track of what it was like to be out in the community doing something positive, to be out in the community without being high.

She pushes the button on the laptop computer, flipping from photograph to photograph on the PowerPoint presentation and reciting the script from memory. She might as well be walking me through a stock market portfolio or a presentation on term life insurance. She's articulate, possesses a command of the facts, and has the kind of poise that I think I *might* develop by age ninety-two. Diane Klenk, her adviser, sits across the table from us and fingers the desk key that hangs on a long cord around her neck. Diane has brown hair and a ruddier complexion, but otherwise she could be Jessica's mom sitting there, or her favorite aunt, watching and commenting from time to time, but letting Jessica speak for herself.

The presentation includes photos of kids working at the local Pamida discount store. They're sweeping the parking lot, washing windows, and stocking shelves in exchange for vegetable seed. Now the photos show Jessica and the other girls planting squash and pumpkins, tomatoes and peppers and herbs. Here they are building a greenhouse, pulling weeds, transplanting seedlings from the greenhouse to the community garden, delivering produce to the food bank. Close-ups picture bushel baskets filled with the deep jewel colors of zucchini and purple cabbage. And here are the girls in their red Skills USA-VICA jackets, looking like any other kids beaming on stage in front of fourteen thousand people.

For the garden of your daily living, plant three rows of peas:
1. *Peas of mind*
2. *Peas of heart*
3. *Peas of soul*

This is the first part of a poem that the girls included in their presentation. Over the years that Diane has worked at the Juvenile Home, she has taken enough kids to USA-VICA competitions to know one simple fact: If your presentation is under seven minutes or over ten, it'll be docked. So when the girls discovered they needed to stretch things out a bit, they added more photos and fleshed out the information. Then they looked at the poem Diane had hung on the vocational classroom wall.

The poem is one of those ephemeral Internet pieces that bounce all over cyberspace with no name attached, no traceable point of origin. One of Diane's friends and fellow Master Gardeners sent it to her, and the girls decided to use it.

Jessica reads it with clarity and earnestness. It sounds like a "Recipe for a Happy Marriage" that might have appeared in an Ann Landers or Dear Abby column more than once. I can't help thinking that at Jessica's age, I would have thought it hokey and embarrassing. It would have been on par with a card that says, "You're beary special," illustrated with a bemused teddy bear holding a heart. But then, that's why Jessica is ahead of the game. She's skipped over cynicism and gone right to gratitude. At eighteen, she knows the value of peace.

Jessica grew up in what some people think doesn't exist: a drug culture in small-town, rural heartland. "There wasn't much to do," she says, "and I fell in with the wrong crowd." Her parents are divorced; her mother's a drug addict. But she was raised by her father and grandparents, who are "good, honest people," she says. In some ways, her life fit the picture of small-town America. She worked at the local Hy-Vee grocery store. She did some baking at home, even a little gardening, although she was more comfortable in the kitchen than she was with a hoe and a spade. But she was impatient. "I'd get tired of waiting for things in the oven, so I'd walk away and they'd burn," she says.

She had her first drink at thirteen. By fifteen, she was smoking pot. Not long after, she got heavily into methamphetamine and other drugs. She dropped out of school when she was a sophomore, and even before that, she didn't attend regularly. Then, still a minor at the time, she ended up at the Iowa Juvenile Home instead of jail to be treated for drug abuse.

"It was the best thing that's happened to me," Jessica says.

Plant four rows of squash:
1. Squash gossip
2. Squash indifference
3. Squash grumbling
4. Squash selfishness

Jessica and Diane are taking me on a tour of campus, but Jessica is the official tour guide. She reminds me of a student ambassador from a college admissions department, the kind who's enthusiastic about the faculty and football team but will tell you the truth about dorm rules and drinking.

The Juvenile Home sits in the middle of a residential neighborhood canopied by big shady trees, not far from the Maid-Rite, Dollar General, and Dairy Queen. The whole town is surrounded by cornfields, and in some places the cornstalks act like they're taking over, standing tall and still so maybe you won't notice.

The brick buildings with light-colored roofs are all lined up around a central green space. On the north side of the square are several buildings known as the cottages. These are the living quarters, providing separate space for boys and girls, about fifteen kids to a cottage.

Jessica is the Daily Organizer, or D.O., of her cottage, a leadership position on par with her role as the oldest juvenile in the home. Of the ninety-one kids here, the youngest is eleven. "This is my cottage," she says with D.O. pride. She takes us inside, where a hall leads past a staff office and into a family room where several girls are punching their hands into the air and kicking up their legs in time with an exercise videotape. A sign over the fireplace mantel reads, WELL DONE IS BETTER THAN WELL SAID.

Jessica points out the laundry room, a back door that's locked at all times, and the kitchen, where the staff and girls receive their meals from the dietary building across the square. The girls work in three crews, Jessica says. She shows me where they stack the dishes, where they set the food when it's delivered, and how they clean up afterward. "We sweep the kitchen and wash it down after every meal," she says. "Even the baseboards. We keep everything sanitary."

The whole place, in fact, is unnaturally dust- and dirt-free. "Every square inch is cleaned every day," Jessica says. This may be a slight exaggeration, but not much. When kids lash out with behavior problems, Diane says, they're assigned extra cleaning duties. "Some of these places are spit-shined," she adds.

Jessica leads us upstairs to the sleeping quarters, where, she says, the girls are on camera all the time. Every night, a staff member sits in a glass booth at the end of the hall and watches a monitor, which automatically switches views from one room to another. Jessica shows no sign of resentment or resistance toward this constant surveillance. Instead, she sounds more like a staff person herself. "This is the Quiet Room," she says, pointing to a space the size of a large closet next to the glass booth. The room is empty save for a cot on the floor, and a window connects it to the booth. "If a girl has behavior problems," Jessica says, "she sleeps in the Quiet Room by herself."

Jessica's room is almost as stark, except for a set of two bunk beds and a cot, each covered with a patchwork quilt. Made by church ladies in the community, the quilts go home with kids who successfully complete their stay. The quilts are the only homey things in the room; a blue plastic storage tub at the foot of the bunk beds holds Jessica's clothes. The room is so sparse, in fact, that a box of tissues sitting on the floor by her bed stands out like contraband.

Kids are on a strict daily schedule here; they ask to use the bathroom, they address staff members only when they're standing in front of them, and they develop three goals each day as part of an individualized overall program. Even though the campus is co-ed, the regular high-school-style classes are not. The academic building has two staircases—one for boys and one for girls—and members of the opposite sex are not to look at each other even as they pass in the hall.

As part of the tour, Jessica shows me two greenhouses, one dwarfing the other. Sitting just outside the academic building, not far from Diane's busy vocational classroom, the smaller greenhouse has been there for years, but the kids outgrew it. The bigger one, which was part of Jessica's presentation, came from a nearby community college, where it had been slated to be torn down. When Diane heard about it, she arranged to have it trucked to the Juvenile Home, and the kids rebuilt it. "I always say beg or borrow, but don't steal," she says.

169

Plant four rows of lettuce:
1. Lettuce be faithful
2. Lettuce be kind
3. Lettuce be patient
4. Lettuce really love one another

When Jessica arrived at the Juvenile Home, the garden project was already under way, governed by the 4-H program. But she got there in time to help rebuild the new greenhouse, a project that took the kids from August through December.

"The staff and I probably could have done it in three

weeks," Diane says, "But we wanted the kids to learn how."

This required superhuman patience. Diane says there were times when she wanted to grab the hammers out of the kids' hands and do it all herself. In the end, the kids gave a Bent Nail Award to the maintenance man, Mel, who consistently showed the most hammer-challenged girls how to do the job, even though some never did get the hang of it.

The kids did all the work, though. They dug holes for the foundation, leveled the site, put the tubing in place, attached the plastic, and landscaped the ground around it. When the greenhouse was ready, the kids started their seedlings, which grew quickly. But they couldn't control the heat inside the greenhouse. They set the plants outside, where they soon were beaten up in a hailstorm. So the kids put up black net over the greenhouse to absorb some of the heat, then they returned the plants inside. There are still beds outside the greenhouse, though, of marigolds, radishes, and beefsteak and Roma tomatoes, all mixed in together.

That's a little how the kids were, too, when they were working on the greenhouse and the garden project. A lot of loners and defiant personalities, all thrown together and told to work toward a common goal.

This was when Jessica started to experience the Circle of Courage, the ideals of the Juvenile Home. A representation of the circle appears everywhere on campus; it hangs in Diane's vocational classroom and in the family room at Jessica's cottage. It's divided into four quadrants: generosity, independence, belonging, and mastery. One of the kids' first jobs each morning is to write in their journals, listing the goals within those four areas that they intend to meet that day. The teamwork of the greenhouse and garden project no doubt showed up in Jessica's journal more than once. She might have mentioned it in terms of stretching the black netting on the greenhouse. Making the structure square. Deciding who was going to weed and who was going to transplant. Writing the script for the USA-VICA presentation and rehearsing it morning, noon, and night.

But Jessica and the other two girls made it work. When it came time for them to go to Kansas City for the presentation, Jessica often had her game face on. She looks at herself in the pictures taken during the trip. "I looked angry," she says, like the user or dealer about to walk out of the kitchen and abandon the cookies still in the oven. But she didn't walk away. She went forward. She went to Kansas City.

No garden is without turnips:
1. Turnip for meetings
2. Turnip for service
3. Turnip to help one another

Showing up is a big deal. Showing up is something Jessica hadn't done much for the past few years, at school, or in life. Showing up was a big step. And she was there, in Kansas City, with the other two girls and their advisers.

This was a bigger deal than we might realize. The girls got to stay in a hotel, where Jessica and Diane shared a room. The girls got to have razors to shave their legs. They got to watch a little TV and spend time by the pool. They got to eat at the Denny's near the hotel, where they endeared themselves to the waiters and waitresses. They got to be out among the general public, where nobody knew where they came from. There were no scarlet letters on their clothes, no green T-shirts imprinted with IOWA JUVENILE HOME. They were just like hundreds of other kids, there to demonstrate their skills in interviewing, parenting, jobs, or community service.

"When you're an addict," Jessica says, "you feel so distant from everybody. But you have to look at it like you have issues, but everybody has issues. The people in Kansas City weren't looking at us as being different, they were looking at us for who we are."

The day they gave their presentation for the three judges, a timekeeper, and about fifteen other observers, Jessica and the other girls waited their turn, sitting on the floor in the hall. Jessica says she was a mess, that her heart was beating a hundred miles an hour. But Diane says you couldn't tell. "She got up in front of the judges and she was so calm," she says.

Everything went right. The girls had rehearsed for countless hours, and each knew her part of the presentation. They talked about the greenhouse, the seedlings, the weeding, the transplanting, the harvesting, the donation to the food bank. They did it within the required time, and they read the poem at the end.

"I knew they'd placed in the competition," Diane says. "I knew as soon as they were done because it was flawless."

A little while later, the announcement came: From among the thirty-five high school and college teams in their category, they'd won second place in the nation. And before long, wearing their red USA-VICA jackets, they got up on stage in front of fourteen thousand people to accept their medals. Unlike the other competitors from all over the country, they had no family in the audience, and they were going back to a place with Quiet Rooms and rules about going to the bathroom. But for that moment on stage, they were like everybody else.

There was another moment, back in Denny's, that was almost as good. The wait staff had taken an interest in the girls and their project, but they, too, didn't know the girls' background. And it certainly didn't matter. After the medal ceremony, the girls chose Denny's for their glory meal. When they showed up with their medals, the wait staff applauded them, right there in the restaurant.

Jessica remembers the moment, the moment of showing up, because she was sober. "It's hard for someone who's not an addict to understand how great it feels to accomplish something," she says. "We were there because we earned the right to be there. Our actions and behaviors led us to that day."

To conclude our garden, we must have thyme:
1. Thyme for each other
2. Thyme for family
3. Thyme for friends

When the girls went back to Toledo from Kansas City, they felt they'd done something great, but there was no heroes' welcome. School scheduling got in the way, Diane says, and a planned celebration assembly was delayed for a week. During that quiet time, Jessica looked at her medals and started to doubt whether the accomplishment was any big deal. But when the assembly finally happened, word of the girls' success got out, and Jessica's small world expanded.

She shows me a red notebook that chronicles the entire project, presentation, and aftermath. It includes photos of the greenhouse and the judges' evaluation sheet from the competition. But it's also bursting with newspaper clippings and letters congratulating the girls on their award. Reporters showed up from all over the state. Letters arrived from people the girls didn't know. Jessica even received letters from her grandmother's lady friends at church back home. "People were thrilled because of what we did," she says.

Jessica will never be without those moments: being applauded on stage in Kansas City, celebrating at Denny's, smiling in front of newspaper photographers' cameras. But she and Diane both know that there are no guarantees about her future. In a couple of days, she's taking off for a long weekend back home in Chariton, and it's clear that she's nervous. She's going to try independent living when she leaves the Juvenile Home for good. And beyond that, she's got some tentative plans.

They involve travel, hopefully to Europe, probably to Paris. "I think the food there is probably great," she says, "and I know the scenery is awesome." She wants to go to college, and then work as a substance abuse counselor.

The garden project expanded Jessica's world beyond the campus of the Juvenile Home, beyond the boredom and fear that led to her addictions. She sounds grateful, and gratitude will probably expand her world most of all. Especially since she looks at herself differently now than she did a few months ago. Winning the competition for the garden project was a piece of that. "I just believed in myself for once," she says. "I looked at it and I saw I'm re-building myself."

Now she may be headed for another kind of challenge, the one that comes when friends look at her success and, instead of saying, "Good for you," say "Why not me?" There's also that nasty and persistent *inner* critic, the one who says, "Who do you think you are? You don't deserve this." But Jessica seems clear about her path. "By helping others," she said as part of the presentation, "the ones we helped the most were ourselves."

It's late afternoon, and she needs to head to the local Hy-Vee grocery store, where she provides job training for her peers. "That concludes our tour," she says to me, sounding like a docent at an art museum. She has a "civilian" shirt to change into, an item from the dime-apiece clothing Diane bought at a Meskwakie Casino garage sale. Jessica says good-bye with her stockbroker courtesy, then smiles her little-girl smile and takes off into the world.

"Water freely with patience and cultivate with love," the last line of the poem reads. Jessica gave it extra emphasis when she read it to me. *"There is much fruit in your garden, because you reap what you sow."*

"We hope she'll be one of our best success stories," Diane says when Jessica's gone. All I know is that, if I were headed to that casino down the road, I'd be willing to bet on her. Mainly because she seems willing to bet on herself.

love story

Live now, believe me, wait not till tomorrow;
gather the roses of life today.
—Pierre de Ronsard

Pauline and Ira Ainsworth are the kind of couple who make you believe in marriage again, if at times you've had your doubts. The birth of their relationship is one of those serendipitous events that seems so finely orchestrated and timed that it can't be called an accident. Even a nun once told Ira, "You two were meant to be together."

Their story is a hybrid of sorts. Part devotion, part purpose, it is a love story that could only happen in a garden. That garden started as a way to memorialize their loved ones who had passed away. But somewhere along the line, between the plants and the music and the food and the Barbie doll that floats in a boat on their pond, it has turned into something much more. Now, their eight acres in southern Maine bring a little vitality to the often-predictable days of elderly people in their area.

It started in 1991, when Pauline was happily married to Roy Faucher, the owner of a small landscaping business in Sanford, Maine. One evening, Pauline and Roy hosted their neighbors, Carolyn and Ira Ainsworth. The men, who had never met before, talked about hunting and looked through catalogs for a new garden tractor for Ira; Pauline and Carolyn chatted about their children and the approaching fall weather. They spent the evening, talked about getting together again, and parted.

Three days later, Ira was reading the newspaper when one of the obituaries caught him by surprise. It was for Roy, who had died of a sudden heart attack the day after the couples got together. He was only forty-four years old. He died on October 12.

Ira's wife, in the meantime, had been having health problems of her own. For fourteen years, Carolyn had been in and out of hospitals and care centers, battling heart disease and diabetes. Ira had come to know what it was like to spend endless days and nights in health facilities, to see them as your second home. Despite his care of Carolyn and her desire to live, she passed away November 12, a month to the day after Roy died.

Two people in happy marriages had lost their spouses within thirty days of each other. Something drew them to one another, leading them toward the next step on the path of their lives. There was a reason Pauline and Ira needed to get together. It was all about planting a garden.

∽

Within a couple months after their spouses died, Ira and Pauline reconnected. Grief became their instant bond, but they also discovered shared interests, like hunting in the dense woods behind their houses. In one of those little ways life has of presenting love in the strangest of places, Ira helped Pauline up to her deer stand just as Roy had done. The two started dating and, in

1993, they married, making a family again for Pauline and her daughter, Yvette.

For Ira and Pauline, it was a fresh start, but their previous lives were not forgotten. Ira moved into the house Pauline and Roy had shared. It's a small home that sits back from the main road, in an area of Maine where moose and bear sometimes weave their way between the houses. Roy's presence was felt in the land behind the house, where he had dug out a pond with a small island in the middle. Between the house and the water sat three piles of clay from the pond, and rangy shoots of grass stuck up here and there. Ira and Pauline had an idea for the land, though, something that motivated them to create a yard of fertile soil.

It was to be a memorial garden, a place to honor their late spouses. Both retired, they would plant flowers and shrubs, and they would open it up to the public so that others could plant a flower for a loved one, too. It would be called Yesterday's Memories Park.

Ira went to work, raking down the piles of clay, covering it with pony manure, and over-seeding with grass. The effort took two years, but finally, the acreage looked more like a park than an unworked field.

Neither Ira nor Pauline had much gardening experience. Ira had worked in the woolen mills and as a painter in a shipyard. Pauline worked for a small manufacturer before caring for her daughter and parents. But the couple bought some perennials, transplanted a few from Ira's old house, and accepted donations from people who wanted to memorialize loved ones. The landscape began to change. That's when something Roy used to say kept surfacing in Pauline's mind. "He loved elderly people," Pauline says. "He used to tell me, 'Children and old people can't take care of themselves. It's up to us to take care of them.'"

This thought led to another: What if, Pauline wondered, they opened up the park to people in nursing homes and assisted-living care centers, inviting residents to come and have lunch, listen to some music, enjoy the flowers, and get a breath of fresh air? No charge. Just bring some hamburger patties and hot dogs or a bag lunch, and let the Ainsworths do the rest.

The couple put out the word to the staff of a local care center, who brought a group for the first outing in June of 1995. It was a success, with food and music and the smiles on the faces of the elderly people who came.

There was just one problem, though. "You need a potty house," one of the aides told Pauline, which is a polite Maine way of telling her that she needed an outhouse, a krybo, a portable toilet. The four hundred feet from the pond-side tables to the house made for a daunting walk to a restroom for people using walkers or canes.

The problem was simple: A potty house costs money. When Pauline found it would cost four hundred dollars to rent it for the summer, she recognized that it was time to get sponsors involved.

Pauline was clear about her intentions, but she had never asked for money before. The thought made her feel queasy. Like Ira, though, she had grown up in the area, and she had a childhood friend who owned a TV store. "If Roland Couture turns me down," Pauline told Ira, "I won't mention this idea again."

Roland didn't turn her down. He listened to her idea, asked her how much money she needed, walked to the safe, and pulled out four hundred dollars. Pauline came home and cried.

"I've had a lot of crying days," she says. She cried when the owner of a local hardware store donated a grill for them to use to cook up the hamburgers and hot dogs. She cried when the same store threw in some bags of charcoal. She cried when Ira built a shed to store all the paraphernalia needed for the outings.

She still cries, especially when she's talking about the outings and the people who come sit under the party tents, tap their feet to the music, and take in deep breaths of the garden's fragrance and the fresh Maine air.

❧

It's a bright July day, with just enough breeze to unfurl the flag on the pole in the center of the park. The Ainsworths, both dressed in jeans and knit shirts, are ready to receive their next guests. Pauline has been working in the yard since seven A.M., setting up all the yard art—placing the frog and gnome by the bridge, the blue gazing ball by the flagpole, and a fuzzy yellow toy duck by a bed of lilies. To protect the items from rain or blowing into the pond, Pauline and Ira set up the yard the morning of each outing and take it down later in the day.

The space is wide open, with plenty of lawn for the canopy tents that Ira and Pauline set up over tables and chairs. But the perimeter of the yard is dotted with vignettes. On a chair rests a baseball cap for the Sanford Mainers, a new ball club whose mascot is a moose. Under a vine-covered arbor is a sanctuary of sorts, with religious figures and a framed saying: SHARED SORROW IS HALF THE

SORROW. SHARED JOY IS TWICE THE JOY. This is a favorite spot for men to come and smoke after lunch, Pauline says.

At one end of the yard is a structure set up to look like a fishing shack, with netting and old cast-iron pans hanging from rusty nails. She and her grandson built it, figuring that they needed a fishing shack to go with the pond. Another display features a memorial for Aunt Jeanette, a local woman who owned a blueberry farm and died at the age of ninety-three. It's not far from the wishing well, a gift that Pauline's daughter gave her soon after Ira and Pauline married and formed a family again.

Among the beds of perennials that link the vignettes around the yard, the showiest flowers on this day stand near the pond. The three-foot-tall lilies and larkspur attract monarch butterflies, which wing their way over to the island, lured by a stand of daisies. The pond and its island, accessible by a ten-foot-long ramp, are the focal point of the park. Groundcover and yews green up the island, where a small structure stands out from the foliage. A doghouse shaped like a church, complete with a steeple on top, is a recent addition to the park. Purchased for ten dollars from a local resident's yard, it received a coat of white paint from Pauline and windowpanes made to look like stained glass from one of her friends.

The church is not unattended, though. On the front stoop is a Ken doll with his arm raised in the air. He is waving at Barbie, who is floating around in a toy boat tethered to the island. They came from the Salvation Army, where Pauline chose the two-dollar dressed dolls over the one-dollar naked ones. "I figured they gotta have clothes if they're gonna be at my church," she says.

⁓

Just before noon, a van pulls up, then an SUV, carrying the staff and residents of Parkview Adult Care Center, a facility located ten miles away. A different group from Parkview has come once a month all summer. Today's eight guests are all women, some with walkers, one in a wheelchair. They gather around a large table and settle in for the next couple of hours. It's a small group. Earlier this week, the Ainsworths hosted sixty people at once. "The buses rolled in, and it was just overwhelming," Pauline says. The musicians, a guitarist and a violinist, have also arrived. They're plugging in to the electrical outlets underneath a nearby canopy.

Pauline is in action, greeting the women, learning their names. The smell of hamburgers and hot dogs breezes over from the grill. Two young boys, the sons of one of the staff members, walk the ramp to the island with their fishing poles over their shoulders; they're trying to catch one of the trout that Ira stocks in the pond. Pauline and Ira pass out cups of iced tea. The flag is flying, and the guests are chatting around the table. The Ainsworths have been doing these outings for seven years, and Pauline says she just gets "higher and higher" every time. The excitement "never wears off," she says.

It's clear that Pauline and Ira have learned by trial and error. Little things, like washing dishes, used to be a problem. What do you do when the dirty dishes are more than one hundred yards from the house? Spread them on a tarp on the ground, then spray them with the garden hose. Ira improved on that system two years ago by building a double sink that stands off to the side of the party area. Solar-heated water from the hose is fed through the spigot then drains into two large buckets underneath. Another little thing was storage. A large storage chest holds some of the thirty-five tarps and canopies used to protect guests from the elements. The new storage building that Ira constructed this year holds chairs, tables, and all the garden ornaments, which used to be lugged to the house after every outing. (One night when the Ainsworths skipped this step, Pauline was up at midnight, rescuing chairs that had blown into the pond.)

Pauline's friend at the TV store continues to pay for the wheelchair-accessible potty house each year, one of the most valuable of all the donations. Pauline equips the kybo with fresh flowers, perfumed hand soap, and a lantern. "People say it's the best one around," she says. But there are other needs for the outings: Plates, cups, napkins, and charcoal need to be replenished several times a year. Electrical cords were a problem until Ira went ahead and purchased them; the greatest need now is a new canopy, since the biggest one has blown off three times this summer in windstorms.

The first year that Pauline solicited sponsors, Ira drove her to different businesses in town. More than once, he drove up to the front door and stopped the car. Pauline took a deep breath, and then crumpled under the stress. "Drive around again," she'd say, and he'd put the car in gear and drive around the block as many times as it took before Pauline was ready to go in and ask for help.

Now her list of sponsors numbers between twenty and twenty-five. Each year, she prepares a report for them with descriptions and photographs of the outings so they can see how their money is used. The reports include the fact that, from late May through September, the Ainsworths host dozens of groups from eighteen different facilities, some from as far as forty-five miles away. Over a four-month period, an average of three hundred people visit Yesterday's Memories Park.

Pauline does something similar for the groups who come to the park for their outings. After their visit, Pauline writes a card, gathers up any photos she took, and she and Ira deliver the package to the facility. "Thanks for coming," the card will say. "Hope you'll come again."

The singer/guitarist taps on the microphone. "I'd like to thank Pauline for having us here," he says. "It's a great day to be alive."

Ira looks at the table of guests. "Every day is a great day to be alive," he says.

You can't overestimate the consideration that Pauline and Ira put into their outings. The vignettes, for instance, take hours to set up and dismantle each outing day, but Pauline wants to make sure all their guests find something to talk about.

Members of the local Garden Club will soon come to identify all the plants in the yard so that the Ainsworths can tag them, anticipating the inquiries of the guests. "I want to tag the plants that people donate so visitors can tell who they're in honor of," Pauline adds.

Over by the pond, near a bed of black-eyed Susans, is a wheelchair, on which the Ainsworths have stenciled, NEED A TAXI? CALL DORIS. The reason, Pauline explains, is that asking for a wheelchair can be embarrassing; calling for a taxi is not.

And on most outing days, Daisy the pony makes an appearance, coming up from the barn to entertain the guests. "She eats potato chips out of the bag," Pauline says. "She'll eat off the table or out of your hand." But Daisy is forty years old, and the music sometimes makes her nervous. Today she's staying in the barn.

As if all this weren't enough, there's also the ice cream. You could take away half the yard art and the smoking sanctuary, but you can't have an outing without ice cream. "These people *live* for it," Pauline says. An ice cream truck normally delivers desserts during the outings, but at times when the truck's been late or hasn't shown up, Ira has been known to make the four-mile drive into Sanford at the last minute to pick up frozen desserts. Now he stocks extras in the freezer just in case of emergencies.

For entertainment after the meal, the Ainsworths offer games tailored to the abilities and interests of their guests. In June, Pauline offered a Father's Day outing for men, who brought their fishing tackle along to try their luck at the pond. Next week she'll be hosting a group of mentally retarded teens, and she'll set up an Olympics for them with bowling, water balloons, volleyball, horseshoes, badminton, and a small pool table. She even sent away for prizes that look like Olympic medals.

For the eight women gathered around the table on this day, Pauline has chosen three games of chance: guessing the number of marbles in a jar, choosing from a fleet of floating rubber ducks to find the one with a number on the bottom, and, the real draw, bingo.

The winners get first choice of several prizes: notepads with floral covers, toothbrushes, necklaces, bars of soap, candy. But there's no chance of losing. "I make sure everyone gets a prize," Pauline says. "No one goes home empty-handed."

When the paper wrappers from the ice cream sandwiches have been picked up and discarded, the dishes have been done, and the games are over, the guests sit back in their chairs, listen to the music, and talk about the reasons they look forward to the outings.

"It's peaceful," one says.

"It's pretty," says another.

"I like being served until the food comes out of your ears," another says.

One had heard of Daisy the pony but was a bit misinformed. "I came to eat with the donkey," she says.

The guitarist and violinist started their set with "Amazing Grace" and followed it with songs in the style of James Taylor or Bob Dylan. The latest is "Have You Ever Seen the Rain?" Under the privacy of the tent, out of earshot of the musicians, the guests are commenting that they like livelier music—Big Band sounds, for instance. "Sometimes they get up and dance," Pauline says. "Even if they're in wheelchairs, they can move to the music." They prefer the musician who normally performs at the outings. He's seventy years old and on oxygen, but his electric organ produces some peppy music.

As the musicians take a break, one of the guests gets their attention. A woman in their group sings and yodels, she says. Her name is Jackie. She is tiny, in a wheelchair, with gray hair falling almost to her shoulders.

"Would you sing for us?" Pauline asks.

"Sure I will," Jackie says.

Ira wheels her over to the musician's canopy, and the guitarist brings a microphone off the stage and sets it in front of her, adjusting it to her wheelchair height. Without hesitation, she begins. "The bells are ringing," she sings, then switches to yodeling for the chorus. Her voice is clear, just a bit quavery, and bigger than you'd think her small body could muster. She is a lone voice on this peaceful day, in the spotlight of the bright sun. When she's done, everyone applauds. "We sing that song at our house," the guitarist says. "We sang it just the other night."

Jackie is easily persuaded to do another number. This time, "It's a Sin to Tell a Lie." She is sitting with her back to her audience, but she's like an artist in a recording studio, intent on her art and the microphone. She finishes with a yodel, and there is more applause.

Ira comes over to wheel her back to her group at the table. "If you ever need me to sing again," she tells the guitarist, "just tell me. I work cheap."

❧

Ira and Pauline know that they may never see some of the visitors again. Some have passed away with their outing to Yesterday's Memories as one of their final experiences.

"Remember the woman who came a couple years ago?" Pauline asks Ira. "She'd been having mini strokes, but the day she came here, she ate and played games. Then she said she wasn't feeling well and they took her to the van to rest. I talked to the staff worker a couple days later and she said, 'Remember that woman? She died later that night.'"

Every visitor to Yesterday's Memories is memorialized in a guest book that Pauline has kept from the beginning.

Page after page of signatures, some scratchy, some elegant, bear witness to the twenty-one hundred guests the Ainsworths have hosted over the years.

"And the thank you cards!" Pauline says, throwing her hands in the air. "I read them over and over." She shows me one of her favorites. "Happy Birthday," it reads. It's addressed to Angie, which offends Pauline not at all. "I remember this woman," Pauline says, understanding how signals can get crossed in a tired mind, and marveling at the effort it took for the woman to put the card in the mail. It came with gifts: two beverage coasters, handmade from squares of plastic canvas woven with yarn.

The Ainsworths' experience with the elderly and infirm has delivered them to a place of boundless compassion.

Ira remembers all the years when his late wife was in and out of care facilities. He remembers the time he spent visiting his brother and sister-in-law in nursing homes, where they sat day after day with nothing to do. He remembers accompanying an elderly group of people on a bus tour once; the director stopped at an ice cream shop but never allowed anyone off the bus.

And Pauline remembers her late husband's dedication to the elderly.

"When people hear about our outings, sometimes they ask, 'What would you want to do that for?'" Pauline says. She nods in the direction of the women around the table, under the canopy. "We do it for them."

It's remarkable enough that Ira and Pauline found each other, thanks to a series of "coincidences" that is not lost on either of them. It's more remarkable still that they have shared the same goals: That Ira could pick up where

Roy left off, turning the pond and island and semicleared land into a park of memorial flowers. That Ira and Pauline could use the land for something that would honor both of their spouses. And that they could share it all, brightening the summer days of hundreds of people each year.

It's as if, when Pauline and Ira made a commitment to each other, they made a commitment to the larger community, too. Destiny seemed to mark their relationship from the beginning, and clearly the Ainsworths have used the marriage as a vehicle for something bigger than the two of them.

"I'll always do this," Pauline says. "I'll always keep the park open for outings. Even if I'm not able to be here someday, the people could come anyway."

Ira looks at his wife like a man who has had his life restored, who's living with a purpose.

"Pauline's enjoyment? I'm with her on that," he says. "I stand with her."

Pauline has that glistening look in her eyes. It could be another crying day. But for sure it's a love story, pure and simple.

gardens that heal

There's something strange going on at the Veterans Medical Center in Asheville, North Carolina. Patients enter the sunny atrium of the ambulatory care center. They take the elevator up to the second floor and check in. They sit down in the waiting area and glance at the TV for a few minutes. Then, while still waiting for their appointment, they get up, take the elevator back down to the lobby, and find a seat near the fountain, as if drawn by an unseen force.

"A lot of times, they don't even know why they do it," says Jill Haynie. But she does. She built the fountain, and she knows it has the power to heal.

Jill has valued the sound of water, the feel of slippery rock, the earthy smell of moss, and the effects of sunlight ever since she was a girl in Georgia, playing in the creek or helping her grandmother garden. After college, she tried working at "real jobs," doing everything from driving an ice cream truck to working for UPS, "I kept trying to do the company thing because my dad had been a company person," she says. "I hated it."

Eventually, she landed a job with a major landscaping company in Atlanta, which maintained IBM's 275-acre property. "We took care of the exterior plants, the interior plants, and hand-pruned everything," she says. "There was detail like you could not believe."

After four years, she decided that, even though the

job allowed her to be outdoors, it was still a job. It was time to go out on her own.

This means that, today, running a garden shop, building fountains and gardens, and doing major landscaping jobs in which she's moving tons of rock, is not classified as work. Neither was building the fountain for the Veterans Hospital.

"I dreamed it," she says. "In the dream, I walked into this space, really smoky and depressing, and I saw a copper bowl. I thought, 'This place needs some feminine energy.' I saw boulders, rocks with moss on them. It was all about balancing the spiritual, physical, mental, and emotional self."

So that's what she built.

The fountain is called Balancing the Grindstone, a salute to the era in which most of the veterans were raised, when hard work and overtime hours were considered the supreme virtues. The base of the structure is an 8½-foot column on which sits a 5-foot-diameter handmade copper bowl. A shorter column rises out of the bowl and is topped by an old millstone. Water runs up through the supporting column, cascades over the millstone and onto rocks in the copper bowl below. The oversized structure is in scale with the atrium, but the sound of the water that runs through it is soft and intimate. Jill built it with her father, a veteran, in mind.

"My daddy missed out on his life because he worked all the time," she says. "I've been kind of a workaholic in my life, too. I think part of me built this for myself."

The fountain was so successful that she was asked to build a meditation garden around it. Working with an artist who does metal ironwork, Jill constructed the garden from a number of unusual items that provide textural interest and the kind of earthiness for which she has a special affinity. They include dry stack rock, an old millstone, a concrete sphere, and a staddle stone, a type of toadstool-shaped stone used in England to keep granaries up off the ground and away from vermin and damp soil. A metal fence surrounds this collection, among which are planted outdoor flowers that Jill hopes will thrive in the Medical Center's sunny atrium.

"I might get some really cool stumps or pieces of wood that have lichen growing on them, too," she says.

The healing nature of gardens isn't something that exists just in Jill's dreams. Therapists and health specialists are discovering—and rediscovering—the ways in which plants promote well-being. Since plants have been shown to lower blood pressure, for instance, landscape architects are planting gardens at hospitals. One program in England introduced gardening in a hospice setting, wheeling the plants to the bedsides of the terminally ill patients. In that program, one woman was growing cuttings for her granddaughter. Knowing they would live on helped her feel at peace about her illness.

In science's effort to prove what we often instinctively know, there are all sorts of studies being done to measure the power of gardens and plants to soothe and calm us. For one study, researchers measured the level of discomfort volunteers felt when they plunged their hands into ice water. Those who were surrounded by plants during the experiment felt less discomfort than those in rooms without plants.

Clearly, plants themselves can be healing, but so can the human interaction that grows from a garden. This past summer, Jill hired two sixteen-year-old football players to move rock. "They started out leaning on the shovel like a city worker, you know?" Jill says. But after three months, they were transformed. Working outdoors in public areas, they became experts when people approached them and asked questions. One of them is now building a pond for his mom, and they both realized that they have options in life beyond playing football. "It built their self-esteem," Jill says.

Like those boys, gardeners may find healing in discovering their own potential. But the healing can come in countless other ways, too, through entering into unexpected friendships, for example, or experiencing unconditional love. If you have any doubt what a garden can do, just walk into anyplace where there's water and light and the smell of wet soil and plants growing.

196   If you need further proof, sit down next to one of the guys in the atrium at the Veterans Medical Center in Asheville. He may not be able to tell you why, but he's there by the fountain, feeling a bit more in balance than before.

truth or dare

A weed is no more than a flower in disguise.
—*James Russell Lowell*

Certain facts sometimes tell us more than we want to know. Take, for example, the fact that one out of every ten Americans is in jail or on probation. That's not a little morsel of truth; it's a big and bitter bite, and it's something a lot of people across the country are trying to figure out. First, why is it that way? Second, how do we turn people around?

One of those turnarounds is gardening.

Cathrine Sneed may know more about the rehabilitative qualities of gardening than anyone on the planet. In the early 1980s, she was employed as a counselor in the San Francisco County Jail. She had started the job with enthusiasm but soon found that encouragement and a new suit didn't keep released prisoners from committing new crimes. Inspired by the book *The Grapes of Wrath*, she decided the prisoners needed a sense of purpose and a connection to the land.

Thus was born what's now known as the San Francisco Garden Project, which started by putting prisoners to work clearing weeds and raising seedlings, and evolved into a post-release program that employs former prisoners and feeds hundreds of people in the community. Sneed's idea seems to have paid off. With an opportunity to do valuable, productive work—especially the work of putting their hands in the soil and watching things grow—many of the prisoners have emerged from jail with their hearts open rather than in permanent lockdown. And it's working. Seventy-five percent of the participants in her San Francisco Garden Project do not return to jail.

This is why gardening has gained a foothold in juvenile justice programs across the country. Catch juvenile offenders while they're young, before the roots of trouble have sunk too deep, and put them in a garden where they can work off some of their aggression, feel useful, and see the fruits of their labors feed those in need.

Many juvenile justice systems are employing gardening now. Each approaches it a bit differently, but the purpose is the same. I took a look at three of them in Pennsylvania, Washington, and California.

❧

When I first heard about the project I was being assigned to, I didn't know what to think. I have some guy I have never met before telling me I'm going to have a half-acre garden. I was thinking, Who the hell am I? Old McDonald?

I really don't remember what day it started or even the month it started in. All I remember is how much I knew I was gonna hate it . . .

—Excerpts from letters of participants in Pennsylvania's first juvenile justice gardening program

In a quiet neighborhood in southeast Spokane, Washington, there's a corner-lot garden that's fertilized with manure supplied by a local alpaca farmer. I find this fact amusing; I'm not sure why. I guess for the same reason that this is amusing to me, too: The seedlings for the garden, which is run by the Juvenile Justice system of Spokane County, are started in a room at the courthouse, under grow lights confiscated in drug raids.

Not everybody has a sense of humor about juvenile justice and gardening, though, and I've just encountered one of them in the alpaca-fed community garden in Spokane. He's fourteen years old, a good-looking kid in baggy jeans and a gray tank top. He looks like the kind of kid who might be playing the tuba in the marching band and praying that he'll grow another foot, except that he's on probation for something—it's not polite to ask what—and he's not happy about working in the garden. "I hate it," he says. "We're doing everybody else's work for them just because we got into some trouble. Terry looks down on us for that."

This is not my experience of Terry LaCoursiere. He's the work crew officer in charge of the garden, a teddy bear of a guy in a Juvenile Justice T-shirt and shorts who seems more like Tony LaRussa than Officer Krupke. He drove the kids in today's crew from the county courthouse to the garden in the Spokane County van, pulling a trailer filled with tools and supplies, and now he's giving them instructions. *Today we're going to build a raised bed for herbs. No, you can't take off your shirt, sorry. Because it's hot and we don't have any sunscreen. I need some of you to start watering the plants. No, you can't roll up your jeans. Same reason. Don't forget to drink water while you're out here. And the strawberries are ripe, so help yourselves.*

Like I said, not exactly a warden kind of guy. Despite the fourteen-year-old's comments, this juvenile justice gardening program doesn't look like backbreaking labor to me. It looks more like a bunch of kids finally getting the attention they deserve.

❧

The same philosophy has been adopted at the Orin Allen Youth Rehabilitation Facility, not far from San Francisco. Formerly a boys' ranch, it's now used as a juvenile facility for teenage offenders from Contra Costa County. The valley in which the facility sits is the picture of the old West, with sweeping fields of green and brown fading at the foothills of mountains in the distance. The main buildings of the campus, however, look nothing like the old West at all. Low and modern, built partly of red brick, they form a complex of classrooms, offices, and dorms, with covered walkways leading from building to building. Flower beds have been added in the last couple of years, brightening the dry landscape. Out front in a large bed, an old tractor sits among the yucca plants as a piece of garden art.

The one hundred boys in the facility have been convicted of everything from misdemeanors to felonies, but no violent crimes. They are here from three to nine months—their behavior determines how soon they get out. They take high school classes. They learn skills in woodworking, bike repair, and cooking. They attend meetings on anger management and Alcoholics and Narcotics Anonymous. They wear blue T-shirts and jeans, they walk single file across campus with their hands folded behind their backs, they sleep in an army barracks-like dorm with cots and lockers. And if they elect to do so, they study gardening with Farmer Dan.

Dan Smith is the part-time garden manager, a bald man in denim overalls and a dark blue T-shirt, who walks the same disciplinarian/guidance counselor tightrope that Terry does in Spokane. Commuting 150 miles a day to work at the Orin Allen facility, he oversees two dozen raised-bed gardens, a small orchard of fruit trees, and the ranch's old three-acre corral, which is now being used for gardening because the land is still ripe with cow manure.

The boys at the facility work in these gardens during morning and afternoon classes, raising food that's used in the facility's kitchen. The idea, eventually, is to turn the place into a small farm, raising enough produce to sell in low-income areas in West Contra Costa County, where residents don't have easy access to grocery stores and fresh food. But they're not quite there yet. Dan and the boys are facing some challenges: intense heat, for one thing, and a biting wind. A cumbersome irrigation system. Crows that Farmer Dan says would rather stare you down than run away. And boys with An Attitude. But they're making progress.

When their small greenhouse collapsed in the wind, Dan claimed an old campus building as a replacement. Long worktables hold plastic trays of seedlings, and grow lights hang here and there from the ceiling. A rototiller sits next to an old pinball machine, and a hand-drawn Farmer Dan poster on the wall shows the current planting design of the raised beds.

One of the biggest challenges of this program is Dan's job description. You just don't see many want-ads calling for a person with corrections experience who also knows the nitrogen needs of green beans. Dan is learning the fine points of gardening, but he knows how to work with the boys. If they swear in front of him, they've got to hit the ground and do push-ups. Two to three dozen of them. They probably won't swear around him again.

"One kid told me I broke him from cussing," Dan says.

These things take time. We always hear that one of the things kids need is consistency. Probably these kids haven't gotten much of that, except maybe consistent criticism or neglect or abuse. That's the great thing about a garden—you have to be in it over a period of time. Like the kids at Orin Allen. Digging in the dirt and shoveling manure in the corral is not going to strip off the layers of armor the first day or the second or even the twelfth. But over time, they're part of something that they start from scratch and see through to the end. How often have they had the chance to do *that*? To feel like they created something? Especially something that could help keep another human being alive?

❧

There was a big empty space where the garden was gonna be and the only thing in it was a huge pile of dirt, a few shovels, a couple of rakes, and a wheelbarrow. As soon as I seen all of that, I knew I was in for a long summer . . .

Pulling weeds was not fun at all. I hate pulling weeds. If I had a garden . . . I'd let the weeds eat the plants, or whatever they do . . .

*Once everything started growing and I started
to think about what we were doing and where all
the food went to, I started feeling really good about
the project. . . .*

In the battle to reclaim kids, many juvenile justice
programs share a powerful weapon: Master Gardeners.
Having passed the equivalent of a CPA exam in horticulture, these gardening experts, many of them retirees, volunteer their time in the community. And many of them
are drawn to juvenile justice.

Barb Johnson is a Master Gardener who volunteers at
the garden in Spokane. She tells me about a conversation
she had with one boy on a work crew a few months ago.

Boy: "I don't know why anybody would want to
garden. We just go to Safeway and buy food. We get corn
in cans."

Barb: "But how does Safeway get that corn?"

Boy: "I dunno."

Barb: "Somebody has to grow it. Without farms and
gardens, we'd have nothing to eat."

Boy: "I guess we'd just eat each other."

These are the kinds of conversations that make you
feel good that Barb is in the garden. She's got the directness of a drill sergeant and the gentleness of a grandmother, and she knows exactly why she's here. She has
volunteered for forty-seven years of her life, and many of
those years she worked in a prison in Spokane. "After a
while," she says, "the prisoners told me, 'We love you, but
you've got to get down to the youth. We've already done
the damage. You've got to get to youth before they end up

here.'" That's when she quit the prison and started helping out with juvenile justice.

Today she's directing the building of the raised herb bed, the watering of the plants, and the planting of pumpkin seeds in little hills surrounded by drainage trenches. Usually, there's a mix of boys and girls, but the six kids today are all male, and they're being cooperative. They picked up all the plastic milk jugs that were turned upside down over the tomato plants to protect them from the unseasonably cool nights, and they've strung up all those jugs on lengths of twine like long plastic Christmas garlands, which will be returned to the courthouse and stored in little cubbyholes in the basement. They've taken turns with the watering can, filling it from the fire hydrant on the corner with water donated by the local water company. Then they hold a stream of water over each plant for a count of one . . . two . . . three, and move on to the next plant.

There's that dichotomy again, that truth versus fiction thing. These kids are acting like they could be the president of Student Council or chairman of Future Farmers of America, yet I know they could be here for ransacking a house or dealing drugs to kids even younger than they are. One boy, tall and gangly, with a few small, discreet tattoos on his arms, talks more than the others and has a bit of dramatic flair. I ask him what he thinks of all this, and in response, he channels the spirit of Eddie Haskell: "I think it's a wonderful idea," he says. "Putting troubled juveniles to work to help the community? I think it's perfect." Two minutes later, I hear him bragging to one of the other kids about how his rottweiler could make a light snack of a pit bull.

Barb Johnson is used to this. She once had to straighten out a black kid who was making disparaging comments about white women. The kid backed down in a matter of seconds. But she recognizes those incidents for what they are. Generally, a bit of swagger and a whole lot of fear.

"You guys are doing good on those hills," she says to the boys crouching down in the dirt with the pumpkin seeds. They are planting three seeds in each hill, covering each one with a bit of sand and soil and patting it in, just like Barb showed them. "They're just fine," she says. "Perfect."

❧

We have moved into harvesting. This is where I got to see why we did this and where everything went. We harvested lots of tomatoes, peppers, corn, beans, and other things . . .

I think for next year all the plants should be staked up and that a fence should be installed to help limit some of the problems we had with rabbits and groundhogs eating all our lettuce and leafy vegetables . . .

On the juvenile justice level, some statistics are clear cut, others are as much a two-way mirror as the kids themselves. Three years ago, the Spokane County Juvenile Community Service Program worked with 130 kids at a time, now it's 476. A lot of that has to do with a better referral system, which makes it possible for parents to get help for their truant and runaway kids before they've committed real crimes. The youths range in age from nine to nineteen, but most of them are between fourteen and seventeen. Youth crime is down, but violent crime is up.

There have been a record number of methamphetamine busts this year. And a lot of the kids come from families who moved to Spokane because their relatives are serving time in one of the county's two state prisons.

Then there's the flip side. The Spokane juvenile justice garden measures about fifteen thousand square feet, and over the past few years, more than four hundred teenagers have helped raise and distribute in excess of ten thousand pounds of produce to local shelters, the food bank, and the Salvation Army. Most of the kids serve between twenty-four and fifty hours of community service time as a condition of their probation. And when it comes time in the spring to gather up seeds and seedlings, the staff and judges down at the courthouse are the first to donate.

There aren't many statistics about recidivism in the juvenile justice programs, partly because, in many cases, gardening is just one of the community service projects in which the kids are involved. In Spokane, for instance, the kids also paint over graffiti at the local skate park and serve food to the homeless at a local shelter. They may, in fact, serve some of the food they've grown.

Maybe, whatever these kids have done—stolen a car, dealt some drugs, broken into a house—maybe they feel that somewhere in that soil, in the alchemy of water and sun, in whatever it is that makes a tomato the size of your fist grow from a tiny seed, that maybe in there somewhere, they'll also find a little forgiveness.

There are no statistics on that.

∽

Sometimes in the search for truth, the best evidence is anecdotal. Sandy Beldon, a retired publishing executive who helped initiate the first juvenile justice gardening program in Pennsylvania in 1995, has proof. From his files of that year, he produces copies of the letters the first juvenile work crew wrote to their probation officers after they'd completed their work in the garden. They each wrote a letter describing their experience and how they assessed it. Was it worthwhile? A waste of time?

This program, one of the first juvenile justice gardening programs in the country, started with the Lehigh County Juvenile Probation Department, which donated produce from the garden to the Second Harvest Food Bank in Allentown. The program became a model for other projects in the state. The first year, the garden grew more than two thousand pounds of produce in addition to flowers and herbs. Within a year, the program spread to five other counties.

Those letters in Sandy's files form an unofficial but candid record of that first growing season, revealing the kids' activities and, more important, their emotions. From what they write, you can almost see them rolling their eyes at the completely uncool idea of planting a *garden*. But by the time they're done, they actually have nice things to say about the whole project. Like maybe it wasn't so bad after all. And maybe they even learned something from it. Here are a few additional excerpts.

∽

There is some things that I would reconsider planting next year, such as the Swiss chard. After all, who eats that stuff that is not a total gardening and vegetarian freak?

It was amazing how things turned out, and how much we harvested. Although it did have its days where I just wanted to go home, it was well worth it . . .

It was a great learning experience for me because I now know how to take care of my plants at home. I give my grandmother advice on how she should grow her tomatoes . . .

I have learned a lot about a lot of things in the past year. I know that I can not change what I did but I have also learned to learn from my mistakes and to live for today. It sucks but I hold on everyday just trying to make it through . . . Anyway thank you for everything that you have done for me. I appreciate it more than you will ever know . . .

Gardening is absorbing. It has a way of engaging and heightening our senses and at the same time calming and soothing our souls. This, of course, is why it's such a perfect balm for juvenile offenders, who are high on energy, and often on anger.

Back in Spokane, Terry LaCoursiere's work crew has been highly cooperative. So much so, in fact, that Terry has told them he's giving them credit for an extra hour of work. Maybe it's my imagination, but they seem calmer, more subdued than when they came.

You look at each of these kids and think, how did he *get* so angry in just fourteen short years? What sort of abuse and neglect hijacked his innocence, even though he still has the baby face? How did he shut down his heart, build a fortress and a moat around it, and put guards at the towers?

And then you realize, oh, the moat—it has goldfish in it, not alligators. And that scary-looking fortress? It's made of plywood, just painted to look like stone. And those are Fisher-Price people in the guard towers, and they're holding toy guns. And then you realize that not only is it an illusion, like the set for *Ben Hur*, but the kid doesn't even *want* it to be real, because he's really still a kid.

That's why the fourteen-year-old who thinks he hates Terry has forgotten that he's the reincarnation of James Dean and is now *skipping* through the garden, right between the rows of tomatoes and squash. Maybe there's not such a difference between four and fourteen after all. Like I said, things can fool you. They're not always what they seem.

Terry knows this. So do Barb Johnson and Farmer 209 Dan and the officials in Pennsylvania and all the people across the country who are putting teenage offenders in gardens. It's like Anna Wasescha in St. Paul told me. Give kids a chance, she said, and they'll tell you what they think. So here's what one kid in Allentown, Pennsylvania, wrote after he'd worked in the garden for a few months:

"I think the program with the garden was excellent for some people and especially for me. Thank you for trusting us."

Now that, I'm pretty sure, is the truth.

kids matter

As the garden grows, so shall the gardener.
—Old Proverb

Pat Williams leads a double life as a gardener. At her home in Yorba Linda, California, an upper-class neighborhood set on the side of a mountain, her narrow slice of backyard overlooks Orange County. The view is so expansive that, from the second-floor window on a relatively smogless day, she can give traffic advice from her bedroom. In the backyard, the view is framed by dozens of rosebushes, a fountain, and birdhouses. There are also birds, dozens of them. Goldfinches cluster around a single feeder and snack on squash leaves in full view of the breakfast windows. Pat knows the birds so well that, if she hears a song she doesn't recognize, she goes to the window to see who's new.

There are squirrels and rabbits, starlings and blue jays, and even coyotes here. Once Pat found a baby possum in the dining room. Yet, she loves them all, no matter how many rose petals or squash leaves they eat. She even loves the hawks, which sometimes swoop down and pick up a mourning dove for a morning meal. It's remarkable, really, how much life there is in this steep suburban neighborhood. "Sometimes the ground just moves with rabbits and squirrels," she says. "My husband gets mad, though, when I start to name them."

About forty minutes away, there's a place that's not so perfect, although Pat is doing what she can to change it. It's the Florence Crittenton Home in Fullerton, which houses sixty kids taken from abusive and neglectful homes. There, a typical day may look something like this:

With her blond hair pulled back, Pat is weeding the garden out back of the facility. She's not alone. A few feet away, a seven-year-old boy is carefully peeking under leaves of squash plants and tomatoes in pursuit of bugs. Another boy, an eight-year-old who's small for his age, is wearing a Pokémon T-shirt and a serious expression, trying to untangle himself from the hose he's pointing loosely in the direction of the carrots and lettuce. A nine-year-old girl's short blond hair sticks out from under the pith helmet she always wears for gardening. And some of the older kids, the teenagers, are working with the younger ones, showing them how to deadhead flowers without disturbing new blooms.

Pat's own backyard, with its saucer-sized rose blossoms and menagerie of wildlife, is stunning. But the scene at the Crittenton home is a miracle. At least, that's how Pat describes it. And she should know. Her vision made the garden grow.

I first talked to Pat years ago, when she wrote to the editor of *Country Gardens* magazine with a story of a garden plot she'd started for the young residents of the Crittenton Home. She sent along three photos that told a story all their own. The first pictured a bare patch of ground tilled for planting, surrounded by a plain brick wall. The next pictured a transformation: the same plot of ground, now a jungle of green, where children stood among beds of yellow black-eyed Susans and marigolds, with sunflowers towering over their heads and a bean tepee nearby.

The third photo, maybe the most telling of all, was a close-up of a white wooden arbor with lattice sides and a curved top. From it hung a sign that clearly had been painted by children. The sign featured butterflies, lady-bugs, a sun, and flowers. And in big colorful letters, it made a proclamation and a promise: THE GARDEN OF FREEDOM.

❧

It was eight years ago, around Christmastime, that Pat first visited the children's home, delivering holiday gifts she'd helped collect from the community. The home was neatly kept, Pat found. But it was lacking something. Out back, the children had a big open area to run and play, but there was nothing to play *on*, nothing to fill up that great expanse of empty space that Pat called "the epitome of nothing."

"Well," Pat thought to herself, "I could plant a garden for the kids."

It didn't matter much to Pat that she wasn't a Master Gardener. An oncology nurse by profession, gardening was something she did for fun. And how much work could it be? Till a small area, put a few seeds in the ground, and help the kids learn to tend the vegetables and flowers.

"I was so naive," she says.

Pat enlisted the help of her husband, Fred, and a

friend, and pretty soon they'd dug up an eighteen-by-thirty-five-foot plot. The first seeds to go in the ground were strawberries and flowers. Once a week, Pat came to the home and gardened with the kids, and the plants seemed to thrive. "They were doing well," Pat says. "They really were."

But then one day, she came and found half the garden dead. "The kids loved to mess with the timer on the water source," she says. Pat had "permanently" screwed it closed, but it had been opened again—with who knows what tool. "I learned fast what it means to have sixty little people with time on their hands," she says.

Pat also learned that these aren't just any little people. These are kids with a whole menu of psychological diagnoses: impulse control problems, attachment disorder, major depression, anxiety disorders, and post-traumatic stress disorder. They range in age from infancy to eighteen years old. Abandoned, born with drug addictions or fetal alcohol syndrome, or removed from abusive homes, they are now wards of the state. With families who are considered unsafe, they can't be returned to their home environments, and they aren't free to be adopted. In short, these are not easy kids. And now they were in a garden. With tender plants. And dangerous tools.

"One kid picked up a trowel and threatened to throw it at another kid's head," Pat says. "They can get mad in a second."

Her reaction was not to give up. It was to find a solution. "I learned that tools demand a high degree of supervision," she says. "Now we only have four or five of them out at a time, and I always know where they are."

Pat talks about these things as if they were no big

deal. That's because, early on, she learned an interesting lesson. "I needed to not be controlling," she says. "If my goal was to have a great garden, this was not it. There are no straight rows, and the kids were snatching seeds out of my back pocket and sticking them in the ground. I didn't know what was planted where."

So what did her goal become? "To let the garden be whatever the kids get out of it. It's beautiful because they made it."

That was a turning point.

Pat recalls a day when she came to work on the garden and met a new boy who followed her around. "Who are you?" he asked. "Do you work here? Are you a social worker?"

Pat told him the truth, that she was there because she liked to garden and that she wanted to garden with the children. "He couldn't accept that," Pat says. "These children couldn't believe that a total stranger would want the privilege of spending time with them." That's why, from the beginning, convincing them otherwise has been the real purpose of the garden.

⁐

Pat has been volunteering at the home long enough now that she's gotten used to this world, so far removed from her own. But every day, her appreciation grows for the people who work here full-time. The kids who come to Crittenton are the ones who "are profoundly troubled," she says. "You have to have a sense of bombproofness to work here."

That, and the kind of compassion that attracts birds and possums to your backyard. One day when a kid made threatening motions with a garden hoe, Pat stayed calm. "If you don't give me the hoe," she said, "you'll have to stop gardening. And I'm having so much fun with you that I'm hoping you'll make the right choice." The key is to not make it a confrontation, she says. "Set it up so the kid can save face." In 99 percent of the cases, she says, the kids will comply.

Over time, she sees changes in the kids who come here. Generally, they're quiet when they first arrive. "They won't say what they want," she says. "They want nothing because they think they *are* nothing." When they talk, she says, you hear the voices of their parents. Eventually, though, they get comfortable and the anger comes out. "It's hard to believe that the sweet child who's thanking you for a new pair of tennis shoes is the one who knocked over the garden shed because she was getting in touch with her feelings."

There's no place better than a garden for that kind of kid, Pat says. "Things in the natural world help bring out things that they're afraid to bring out on their own. You see agitated kids quiet down. It's a whole lot better than medication."

215

꧁ꙮ꧂

The Crittendon staff keeps a scrapbook of the home's activities. One photo shows a little girl in purple pants and a white top with hearts and flowers. She's holding a blue ribbon from the Orange County Fair, and the ribbon is almost as big as she is. The children won four ribbons for their flowers, including one for a huge yellow dahlia. Pat went to the store and bought blue ribbons for everybody to mark the event. This was major progress.

When Pat first started gardening with the children, the plants were picked clean daily. If a zucchini started to form, it was plucked by curious fingers. If a green pepper appeared, it was a goner, picked by a child on eye level with the plant.

"You know," Pat told the children, "one of the most important things to have in a garden is patience."

The kids didn't get it. Patience? They'd never seen it before. What did it look like? What was the point? They were used to parents who hit first and thought later. What did patience have to do with anything?

"It has to do with pumpkins," Pat told them.

There's something magical about a pumpkin. So big, so round, so *orange*. A vegetable you can sit on. Kids are mesmerized by pumpkins. Pumpkins were the perfect lesson in patience.

They planted several the first summer. When they bloomed, Pat held her breath. A couple of the blossoms disappeared. Then a couple of the little pumpkins disappeared. But one pumpkin, tucked under a leaf, continued to grow. It grew and grew, and every week Pat reminded the kids: "Sometimes taking care of something means just letting it grow. Let's leave the pumpkin alone and see how big it gets."

The kids listened, leaving the pumpkin untouched for an eternity of 120 days. When it reached maturity, Pat and the kids celebrated their major accomplishment. "I was amazed," she says. "It made me realize how far they've come."

From that initial pumpkin, they've advanced not only to the county fair, but to a Food for Friends program, too.

Pat set it up, helping the kids harvest vegetables for the city's food bank to feed the hungry. "It allows the children to give back to the community," Pat says. "They get to step out of the victim's role."

∽

Pat doesn't play favorites with the kids, but she can't hide the fact that she felt special affection for a boy we'll call Ricky. No one's sure, but he may have had fetal alcohol syndrome; certainly there were signs of it in his face, which was scrunched up like a wise old man. He wore glasses and sometimes a patch over one eye.

During his years at Crittenton, he was by Pat's side, having gardened with her since she dug up the first plot. When Pat came to spend time with the children, he ran at her out of sheer joy, like a puppy jumping and spinning in circles.

One day, Ricky glanced at the chrysanthemums poking out of the ground, then looked around like something was missing. "Where's the Miracle-Gro?" he asked Pat. "Aren't you gonna fertilize these babies?"

This was the same kid that Pat described as "quiet, with an inner voice. The perfect kind of kid to garden with." He picked up each plant lovingly, she says, holding it in his hand and inspecting it before he set it in the ground. His appreciation of each leaf, each petal, was evident. If the flower were a dog, he'd be scratching it behind the ears.

Pat told me a story about wallpapering Ricky's room. The Crittenton Home was once a hospital and still felt cold and sterile. To warm it up, Pat asked local businesses to sponsor a child's room, donating enough money to buy a wallpaper border and coordinating bed linens for each one. Ricky was getting a Star Wars room, with a wallpaper border of stars and planets.

"When I started on his room," Pat says, "it was late in the day, and I only had time to put up the border on one wall before I had to leave. The one strip was behind his bed. Ricky told the staff that he thought this was all the border he was going to get, and he wasn't unhappy about it. That night when he went to bed, he stuck his pillow at the foot of the bed so he could look at the border as he went to sleep. He said it made him think about God watching down on all of us.

"Ricky may have lots of problems, but he's a very deep little kid," she adds. "He sees God everywhere."

One day, when a reporter visited Crittenton to see what the garden program was all about, the home's PR person was going crazy, Pat says. Kids were everywhere in the yard and around the garden, and most of them were just a bit out of control. Ricky saved the day. He was planting flowers, and when the reporter asked him what he was doing, he said, "Taking care of God's little creatures."

Pat's personal philosophy has developed along with the garden, and now it's so simple that she had it printed on her license plate: KIDSMATTER. That's also the new name of this garden: Kids Matter Park, which encompasses all of what the garden has grown to be. Still a garden of freedom, it is now much more, including a picket fence, playground equipment, and benches with hand-painted tiles, all donated by local groups who heard about Pat's efforts and wanted to help. "When the piece of playground equipment arrived," Pat says, "it was more exciting than when my husband and I bought our house."

Over the years, one of Pat's most loyal volunteers has been David Gardner, a local landscaper. "He's the most shameless solicitor I've ever seen," Pat says. Because he knows everybody in town, he's gotten $1,800 worth of irrigation lines laid for free, not to mention other fix-ups that would have cost thousands of dollars in donations. One day, Pat pointed out a tree that needed to be removed. David pulled out his cell phone and called a tree-trimmer friend of his. "Here's the next thing you're going to do for free for Crittenton," he told his friend. "They need a linden tree removed. It'll be good for your soul. And I heard you just bought a Miata, so I know you don't need the money."

For the first few years, Pat and other volunteers could just drop in any time and garden with the kids. Now, new laws require formal therapeutic programming for most of each child's day. While Pat possesses natural abilities in working with kids, she is not a therapist, and at first she was a bit irritated with the new rules. "What am I going to do?" she says, "ask these kids, 'What were you *feeling* when you were digging in the dirt?' Or, 'When you ripped the tulip's head off, were you thinking of your mother?'" Fortunately, the laws have had their upside. "Now, more staff are gardening along with me," she says.

With Pat's persistence, it's no wonder this garden has thrived. "Be very gentle," Pat tells a five-year-old girl who is new to the home and the garden. The child's hands, purposely ungloved so she can feel the plant's delicate roots, are covered with dirt. "Pick up the plant like this," Pat tells the girl, "and tickle its feet." At that, she shows the girl how to spread the plant's roots before setting it in the ground. "And now," she says, "we tuck it into its bed." In seconds, another chrysanthemum is in place, with a few trowels of dirt patted around its stem.

"The garden is a symbol of permanence," Pat says. "These kids have been yanked out of their homes, and they have no control over their lives at all."

Any number of things could happen next. The garden hose could be flung over a branch of a tree and turned into a swing. The three green peppers that were attached to a plant and growing just a minute ago could be gone. Or the kids could go wild harvesting potatoes. "Talk about digging for gold," Pat says.

She shakes her head in wonder. She seems in no particular hurry to get home to her roses. "Gardening doesn't take a lot of money or volunteers," she says, "and it can make a difference because it's so personal." She wipes her dirty hands on her jeans. "Every day, I see five-year-olds who have had horrible lives. I hope that, for a little while, digging in the dirt can help them forget the bad stuff."

grace from
the garden

One is nearer God's heart in a garden
than anywhere else on earth.
—Dorothy Frances Gurney

Earlier this year, my mom was admitted to the hospital for a heart attack. At eighty-seven years old, she's been a stranger to hospitals ever since she had triple bypass surgery in 1982, but she'd had frequent spells of angina, so the trip to the hospital was not unexpected. The heart attack passed, and by the time the nurses settled her into her room, the nitroglycerine had kicked in, and she was feeling like she'd just as soon be at home, where she knew she could salt her food as much as she wanted. The doctor elected to keep her in the hospital to monitor her condition and medication, though, so a nurse wheeled a computer into her room and walked her through the long list of admissions questions. I sat by with my brother Mike and his wife, Sue, and we all tried to behave.

"Do you have arthritis?" the nurse asked.

"No," said my mom.

"Any history of diabetes?"

"No," said my mom.

"Any respiratory problems?"

"No."

"Do you drink alcohol?"

Mike answered for her. "Once every twenty years," he said. "But she's missed the last two times."

"Do you smoke?" the nurse asked.

"Only when she drinks," Sue said.

"Do you use a walker or a cane?"

We all smiled at this one.

"Actually, we try to discourage her from cleaning out her own gutters," Mike said.

The nurse started to get it.

We didn't tell her that when my mom was about eighty-two, she and my sister, Kathy, lifted a hundred-pound tree stump into Kathy's car and rolled it into my mom's yard, where my mom positioned it, set a sundial on top, and surrounded it with daylilies. When my mom was eighty-three, Mike succumbed to her requests and showed her how to use a chain saw so she could trim out some dead wood from her shrubs. At eighty-four, she laid a new brick border along her perennial beds, which seem to expand every year.

So it was quite a shock, just three days after my mom was admitted to the hospital, that her condition seemed to be worsening. She looked her age for the first time, her skin and her hair had lost their vitality, and she was dwarfed by five huge pillows keeping her in a semi-comfortable position. She winced with pain whenever she moved and couldn't get out of bed without help. She and Mike had started talking about home nursing care.

We should have known better than to worry. By the

end of the day, after she'd decided to schedule an angiogram, been removed from a double dose of blood thinner, and eaten an ice cream bar that Mike sneaked in from the hospital cafeteria, the color returned to her cheeks, and she sat up and belly laughed. We think it was the ice cream bar that did it. But whatever it was, she was home two days later. Without the angiogram. She decided she didn't need it.

My mom has the mark of the phoenix, that perpetual ability to rise and rise again, never acknowledging the possibility of defeat. We attribute it to her positive attitude. It's something the whole family —children and grandchildren—acknowledged when she turned eighty and we put together a book of letters, stories, and poems for her. The memories in the book generally fell into three categories: her quilts, the Sweet Petal rolls she makes for Christmas morning each year, and her garden.

꧁ ꧂

My sister, Kathy, and I have the same childhood memory, probably of the very same spring. Despite having several children at home, my mom would get up at 5:30 on spring and summer mornings so she could spend time in the garden before we awoke and disrupted any possibility of peace. The backyard of the house, the same house where she still lives, was long and fenced, with perennial beds all around the perimeter. One spring, the spring when I was in seventh grade, my English teacher was leaving to have a baby, and my class was having a going-away party. I wanted to take flowers to school.

My mom went out to the yard with a sharp knife and a wet rag and started cutting. The bouquet wrapped in that rag grew and grew. In my mind's eye, the bouquet is enormous, with bright red tulips, light and dark purple irises, white daisies, stems of hollyhocks and gladiolas, poppies in the deepest possible orange, fragrant roses in pinks and yellows, and a few stems of lavender lilacs thrown in for good measure. Now, looking back, I'm sure this is a blended memory, arranging all the favorite flowers of youth in one symbolic bouquet. But then again, Kathy remembers the same thing. At the very least, there were beds of flowers bursting with color, continuing until the first hard frost of fall.

These are things I didn't fully appreciate until I got older, just like I didn't understand what a steadying presence my mom was for people outside our family. Several of my friends had mothers who locked them in closets or berated them until they ran away in self-defense or made them feel about as loved as a piece of burnt toast. In contrast, my mom's worst character flaw is that she always, *always* wants to do whatever *you* want to do, which can drive you crazy for sure, but in the grand scheme of things isn't much to complain about.

One friend came home from college with me for a weekend and witnessed this exchange between my mom and my brother Jim:

Mother: "Would you mind running to the store for me?"

Jim: "Sure. What do you need?"

This turned my friend's world upside down. She had a dad and three brothers, and her mom didn't get much respect from any of them, so she wasn't used to cooperation. "It's so easy," she said, looking like someone had just shaken her awake.

That's when I started to get it.

My mom has always made life look easy. Not that it always has been. Sometimes I think of how long a life she's lived. She was born at a time when she and her sister had to carry water from the stream to the house in pails, and they wore bonnets and once picked cotton in the fields of Arkansas. She worked at a state office job during the Depression, processing letters from people pleading for five or ten dollars so they could feed their children. From my childhood, I remember her down in our basement, using a wringer washer to do laundry for eight, and sprinkling water on my dad's handkerchiefs so they would steam when she ironed them. And now, in the past few years, since life has become more leisurely, she has entertained herself by pulling up a chair to a Compaq computer Kathy gave her and playing every one of the program's Free Cell solitaire games. All thirty-two thousand of them. She played them in order. She kept track.

When she was eighty-four, I realized that I was half her age. I was also the age she was when I was born. For years, I perceived this as a vast difference, not so much in number of years as in cultural experience. I can remember the summers of my adolescence when I would lie out in the backyard near the flower beds. I stretched out on a blanket with baby oil all over my body, which has, to this day, never known a tan. My mom would stand at the back door, up by the hollyhocks, and call to me, "Don't stay out there too long." I could tell she was fretting. "Don't get burned." And then, not wanting to insist that I come in and save my skin, because she is not one to tell you what to do, she would whip up a cake or chocolate chip cookies, then stand at the back door licking the spoon and letting the aroma float out from the kitchen in my direction, knowing that she had won.

One time, she suggested I wear a bonnet when I went out in the sun. A *bonnet*. It was 1970, and she was making fur vests for my brothers and sisters to wear with their love beads, and she was suggesting that I wear a bonnet. This was when I thought, possibly, we would never understand each other, that there were too many years between us. But somewhere in the last thirty years, my perspective has changed. She still may not be the person I most want to talk to about something like sex, but honestly, how many moms are? The point is, she taught us a lot. One of the things she taught me is that, as long as I didn't use it to scorch myself, the garden is a healing place.

❦

226   Two years ago, my dog Sabra died in early March, leaving me with a broken heart. I was single, ending a relationship, and coming to a crossroads in my work. And now Sabra, a malamute who had been my constant companion for eight years, had died of lymphoma, just three weeks after her diagnosis.

We had an early spring that year, so just days after Sabra died, I entered my garden. I opened up a whole new bed, along a side of the yard that had once been reserved for her dog run. I planted sweet woodruff and lily bulbs, made a border of hostas, and added purple coneflowers and miniature pink roses. As I dug in the dirt on my hands and knees, I repeated a mantra: *I love this plant like I love Sabra.* I did it over and over with every plant my hands touched. I blessed the earthworms with it, I blessed the soil, I repeated it until I drove sadness from my mind and replaced it with peace.

I did it knowing that this was the kind of energy my mom had often brought to and received from the garden.

That year, my garden bloomed like my mother's always has. It was an endless parade of color, including the dark purple iris my mom had given me. But the plant that turned heads was the climbing rose next to the back door. I had tried to dig it out by the roots years before, as it had only bloomed once. But this spring, the spring I loved my garden the way I loved Sabra, that rose put on hundreds of blooms, a mass of deep red, climbing up the trellis and onto the second floor of the house. Inside one day, I looked at the bush through the windows on my back porch, and I realized it had a message for me. Two prominent canes were twisted around each other in the shape of a heart, through which the sun shone and made the roses glow.

This is when I learned what my mom has always known: The life energy that brings flowers into bloom will carry a garden a long way. But give those flowers even a bit of unconditional love, and they can achieve their full potential.

∽

On Memorial Day, a week after my mom came home from the hospital, her peonies burst open. Like others of her generation, she has always considered them Decoration Day flowers, so their timing was perfect. They are a bright purplish pink with yellow centers and flat separate petals, and I forget how vibrant they are from year to year.

They are my favorite flower because when I was little, a bank of them grew behind the swing set. In late May, as I swung on the swing, I smelled their fragrance and pretended it was exotic perfume.

I know people who consider peonies a waste because they shatter so easily in spring storms. But my mom and I are alike in our appreciation of them; the momentary explosion of color is enough. It may be romantic and frivolous, or it may be the meaning of living in the moment—I don't know. I do know that if spring flowers bloomed all the time, we'd take them for granted, maybe not see them or smell them at all.

At dusk on this Decoration Day, we sit in the backyard and look at her flowers. My mom has been able to do nothing in the garden this spring; her neighbor mowed the lawn, but otherwise, the plants have been on their own.

228

They are perfect.

A border of lamb's ears edges the beds all the way around the back. Their soft grayish color complements the deep purple iris, the ones passed down from my grandmother to my mom. Flowering almonds stand in the back with their lacy white blooms, and the hostas over in the shady corner are uniform in size. It is the childhood memory of garden abundance, a healing spot if there ever was one. My mom has not been able to tend the garden, so the garden is tending itself.

She's stretched out on the lounge, looking up at the wispy leaves of the locust tree. The crickets have started to sing.

"Did I ever tell you what we used to do with June bugs when I was a girl?" she asks.

"No," I reply.

"We used to tie a string around one of their legs and fly them like a kite," she says. "Then we let them go."

⌘

My mom has always believed in the supernatural. My dad believed, too. I think this is part of the reason they weathered so many changes in life with such apparent grace, because they paid attention to the constancy of nature and its unseen forces, looking for answers and accepting them when they came.

My dad died thirteen years ago, at the age of eighty-four. One day he was out pruning the plum trees in the front yard and feeding the goldfinches in the back; the next he was in a coma from a heart attack and breathing with the help of a respirator. Three days went by, and it was clear he wasn't coming back. We had to make a decision about keeping him on life support or removing the respirator and letting nature take its course.

We sat around a table in the ICU. My mom propped up her elbows and wiped her eyes from time to time with an embroidered handkerchief that was rumpled and wet. Several of us kids sat with her. We all knew our dad wouldn't want to have his life prolonged, but it was our mom's decision to make. "I just wish I knew about his soul," she said, "whether it's gone on, or it's still with him here."

We decided to take a break to rest and think, then we met back at the hospital after lunch. It was only two hours later, but for my mom, it seemed that everything had changed. The light in her eyes had returned, the lines in her face had smoothed, and she leaned back in her chair with a sense of peace.

She had gone home, she said, to the acreage she and my dad owned. She lay down on her bed, closed her eyes, and asked for guidance. A few minutes later, she heard a racket at the back of the house, so she got up and went to the bay windows overlooking the yard. "I couldn't believe it," she said. "There were goldfinches. Hundreds of them." She told us how they swooped and played in wide circles around the yard, right over my dad's vegetable garden. They weren't lighting on the feeders. They weren't fighting for food. They just flew and sang, and after a couple of minutes, they were gone.

"That's when I knew," my mom said. "It's okay to let him go."

❧

When my mom entered the hospital in May, I went into the garden. It was our first spring on the land my husband, Bob, and I bought the year before, and I didn't have a garden plan. I just knew that I needed to dig in the dirt and get something rooted.

Through the summer, though, Bob and I traveled a great deal, so I had little time to keep the flowers going through the heat and drought. Without the kind of relationship my mom has built with her perennials, mine suffered from a failure to thrive. Still, by July, the lushness of summer had established itself unaided, and my mom was holding her own.

One day I sat outside on the glider under a grove of trees, writing. A woodpecker was at work on a tree nearby, and Wolf, our gigantic German shepherd/malamute, looked up in curiosity. Two white butterflies danced around at the back of the yard in the underbrush. The thicket of cottonwoods and multiflora rose and vines and half-grown mulberry trees looked a bit mysterious, as though they could be habitat for fairies or Bigfoot, depending on your frame of mind. I thought of Trudi Temple in Chicago and figured those little white butterflies *do* have a bit of a brain. At least they had enough sense to be in our yard and not in the death trap of her net. We'd had rain, several inches of it, and we'd witnessed the advance of dramatic thunderclouds that darkened the sky and then left the landscape cleaner and clearer than before.

Wolf grazed, ripping grass out of the ground as if he hadn't eaten for days. The neighbor's horses wandered down to our back pasture and stood flicking their tails back and forth and kicking to shoo the flies away.

Life felt peaceful again, the way it feels when there are light breezes and good sleeping weather.

In the looking-glass clarity of such peaceful, sane moments, I can see that we stir often up trouble to make life interesting, and to grow. We were talking about this at our *A Course in Miracles* study group meeting recently. Stephen, a geneticist for a seed company, likened our human experience to a spiritual gymnasium. The place is filled with equipment, he surmised, and we have to keep advancing to more challenging workouts as a way to grow. We choose, sometimes consciously, sometimes not, to put ourselves in crisis situations. Partly to serve, partly to learn.

What would life be like, we wondered, if we had mastered all the equipment, if there were no new spiritual aerobics in the form of challenges and self-doubts? Boring. That's what we decided. It's curious that we don't learn from peaceful moments as we do from arduous ones, but we don't. I guess that's why gardens are such places of respite and repose. Because we know that no matter how much we love the peace and quiet, we're still going back to the gym.

❧

Now it's early September. My mom has not returned to the hospital. "The doctors sent me home to die," she said to me recently, "but I showed *them*." Still, her angina flares often some days, and she moves more slowly and unsteadily. She seems to be shrinking at a more rapid pace, and I feel like a professional wrestler when I hug her, she is so tiny.

One evening when I go to visit, we eat pizza and play Rummikub, but most important, we stand at the back door and look at the yard. A windstorm last week felled the privacy fence that separated her yard from the neighbor's behind her. It had stood there for at least thirty years. The neighbors, whom she had never met, hauled it away and told her they don't intend to replace it. So now her yard is just one half of what, overnight, has become a small park.

"I'll enjoy looking at their flowers," she says. I think they will enjoy hers even more.

We look out the front door, too, at the empty space next to the stoop where Mike removed a dying evergreen that was there before I was born. "I don't know what I'll plant there next spring," she says. "Any suggestions?"

She's thinking of the next planting season, and for this I'm grateful. I'm grateful that she's able to be at home, shuffle the cards, open her own can of tuna, eat an ice cream bar, change the channels on her own remote control. I'm also grateful that there's a plan we cannot see. It keeps us on our toes, reminding us to breathe a peony's perfume while we can.

I worry about her after this visit, but the next night, in her phoenix-like way, she calls and leaves a message. "I'm feeling good," she says, sounding youthful again. "No pain today."

My mom and her garden have always put things in perspective. They've shown me that time is not finite. That grudges, even if they take root, produce nothing. And most important, that the spirit lives on.

My mom may be here for years, or she could be gone in a matter of days. But in truth, she will live forever. Next year, right on cue, her peonies will fill the yard with fragrance, and her purple iris, the ones passed on from generation to generation, will continue to grow. A new redbud tree will present itself, or a few more of my dad's wildflowers will appear in some new and unexpected spot.

Her ground is like that: fertile soil, in which new plants keep popping up and reaching for the sun.

appendix: resources

To follow up on any projects in this book, contact the people and Web sites listed below. I've included a few tips to help you with gardening and with planning ways you can change the world one garden at a time.

gardens that teach

⋒ good questions

Will Allen offers a number of workshops and training programs for people interested in urban gardening, setting up community food centers, and working with children. For more information, visit **www.growingpower.org**, or contact Will via will@growingpower.org.

Urban Community Gardens is an organization that can help you identify funding sources and make contacts in setting up urban gardens. There are many sites on the Web that provide more information. Visit **www.foodsecurity.org**, then click on Links, to find just a few.

For more information on the Heifer Project, please visit **www.heifer.org**.

* wild one

Virginia Umberger belongs to Wild Ones—Natural Landscapers, Ltd., a nonprofit with a mission to educate and share information with members and the community at the "plant-roots" level, promoting environmentally sound gardening practices and landscaping using native species. For information, visit **www.for-wild.org**.

Virginia also has been active in the American Gourd Society, which promotes interests in gourd cultivation, history, and crafts. Visit **www.americangourdsociety.org** for more information.

If you're interested in gourd decoration and crafts, Virginia recommends books by Ginger Summit and Jim Widess, including *The Complete Book of Gourd Craft: 22 Projects, 55 Decorative Techniques, 300 Inspirational Designs* (Sterling Publications, 1998), *Gourd Crafts: 20 Great Projects to Dye, Paint, Carve, Bead and Woodburn in a Weekend* (Lark Books, 2000), and *Gourd Pyrography* (Sterling Publications, 2002).

* interplanting

Priscilla Logan has developed a program that trains teachers on setting up and using outdoor classrooms. She would be happy to share information on this or the wetlands project. Contact her at **plogan@outdoorclassroom.org** or visit **www.outdoorclassroom.org**.

gardens that nourish

* heaven and earth

Jim Call is eager to help communities across the country start their own GardenAngel program. Contact him by visiting **www.casagarden.com** or at **jimcall@casagarden.com**.

Additional information is available through the CASA (Care Assurance System for the Aging and Homebound) office in Huntsville, Alabama, at (256) 880-0603 or by visiting **www.casamadisoncounty.org**.

* greetings from rocky roost

Julie Williams would be happy to talk with you about gardening, art, and children. Contact her at **rockyroost@arkansas.net**.

* remembering

For details about the Portland Memory Garden, including upcoming training sessions on designing and building a memory garden for people with Alzheimer's, visit the Center of Design for an Aging Society at **www.centerofdesign.org**, or call Eunice Noell-Waggoner at (503) 292-2912.

Worth County Primary School has received several state and national honors for its innovative programs. For details, visit **www.peanut.org**; click on Our Schools, then on Worth Primary. Or call (229) 776-8660.

gardens that unite

* gardener without borders

For more information about Dr. John Wilson's efforts to build greenhouses in Korea, contact him at **jkwndw@aol.com**.

The Web site for Christian Friends of Korea also includes information about the work in Korea. Visit **www.cfk.org**.

* mother tongue

For more information about Farm in the City, visit **www.farminthecity.org**. Anna Wasescha has developed a number of strategies for building support for community garden projects. For example:

- Shop your community for land. Vacant lots can be threatened by development, so look at high schools, colleges, parks, community spaces, and hospitals. Remember that community gardens can be any shape and size.

- Encourage homeowners near your garden to dress up their own property. Neighbors are more likely to stop and talk if they see you gardening in your front yard, Anna says. "A garden is a reason to talk to somebody else. It's the way you build social capital."

- Remember that most gardeners are generous people and will share their plants, seeds, compost, wood chips, and clippings for free. Look for ways to get resources without any expense.

- Consider all possible funding sources, including arts organizations, local booksellers, corporations, banks, etc.

* we the people

Complete information about the Clinton Community Garden is available online at **www.clintoncommunitygarden.org**.

The Clinton Community Garden is a member of the American Community Gardening Association (ACGA), which is a national nonprofit of professionals, volunteers, and supporters of community greening in urban and rural communities. Contact ACGA by calling (215) 988-8785, e-mailing **smccabe@pennhort.org**, visiting **www.communitygarden.org**, or writing to

100 North 20th Street, 5th Floor
Philadelphia, PA 19103-1495

For more information about the Trust for Public Land, contact the national office, located at 116 New Montgomery Street, 4th Floor, San Francisco, California, 94105, call (415) 495-4014, or visit **www.tpl.org**.

For information on funding resources for community gardens, visit **www.hort.vt.edu**. Once you're there, click on Research and Extension, scroll to the bottom and click on Human Issues in Horticulture, click on Community Gardening, then select Community Gardening Resources.

gardens that inspire

For information on gardening with disabilities, contact the American Horticultural Therapy Association by visiting **www.ahta.org**.

* market day

Information about Trudi Temple's Market Day fundraising cooperative is available at **www.marketday.com**.

* fresh start

For more information about SkillsUSA-VICA, a national organization that serves trade, industrial, technical, and health-occupations students, visit **www.skillsusa.org**.

Diane Klenk and the staff at the Iowa Juvenile Home also work in conjunction with 4-H programs. For more information about that organization, visit **www.fourhcouncil.edu**.

* love story

To contact Pauline and Ira Ainsworth for more information, call them at (207) 324-8466. If you're interested in offering outings in your community, take advantage of these tips from them:

• Choose a location that will be easily accessible to vans and people with walkers and wheelchairs. Make sure a handicapped-accessible restroom is within short walking distance.

• Identify the retirement, assisted-living, and adult daycare centers within an hour of your location. Visit the centers in person to invite staff members and clients to your outings.

- To cover the costs of tables, canopies, food, and other materials, solicit the help of local businesses as sponsors. Provide sponsors frequent reports of the outings so they'll know how their money is being used.
- Protect your investments by storing all materials carefully and keeping them out of the elements. This will help your sponsors know that you're a responsible steward of their money.
- Keep the outings menu simple. Grill hamburgers and hot dogs, for instance, and serve watermelon, iced tea, water, and ice cream.
- Make arrangements for live music and games.
- Keep a guest book for a record of all the people who come.

gardens that heal

Jill Haynie's Web site, **www.theenchantedgarden.net**, offers information about her fountains and other landscaping projects, as well as merchandise in her store, The Enchanted Garden. Contact her by calling (866) 210-4521 (toll-free) or (828) 669-0017 or by writing her at

The Enchanted Garden
104 Broadway Street
Black Mountain, NC 28711

For more information about the healing power of gardens, contact the American Horticultural Therapy Association by visiting **www.ahta.org**. This nonprofit organization promotes the use of horticultural therapy with people who are physically disabled, mentally ill, elderly, substance abusers, and terminally ill, among others.

✳ truth or dare

For more information about the juvenile justice gardening program in Spokane, Washington, call Terry LaCoursiere at (509) 477-6381. An overview of Spokane's entire juvenile justice program is available at **www.spokanecounty.org**. Click on Government Index, then Juvenile Court.

Just for fun, here's a gardening tip from Barb Johnson, the Master Gardener who volunteers in Spokane: When you're transplanting a seedling, put some of the original soil in a cup and mix it with enough water to make a slurry. Pour this around the transplanted plant in the new location. The original soil has bacteria in it that helps the plant take in water, Barb says. She does this all the time with consistent success, even when moving plants from one part of the country to another.

For more information about the Orin Allen Youth Rehabilitation Facility and the East West Garden Project, visit **www.ccprevention.org**. Or contact Melody Steeples, program manager for Community Wellness and Prevention Program at Contra Costa Health Services, at (925) 313-6839 or **msteeples@yahoo.com**.

* kids matter

Pat Williams has compiled "Thoughts on Gardening with Abused Children." For her complete list, and for more details about her work at the Florence Crittenton Home, call her at (714) 779-1714. Here's just a sample of practical suggestions:

- Locate the garden away from play areas where kids and balls fly, if possible.
- Drip irrigation on timers works great. Kids can always do hand watering, but it's disaster in the making if you rely only on hand watering.
- Contests are great. Have kids guess how tall the tallest sunflower is, how much the giant zucchini weighs, etc.
- Arrange for their flowers or vegetables to be in local fairs.
- Don't use pesticides. Know that kids will be eating veggies off the plants.
- Kids like to have "their own" plants. Big seeds in individual pots are fun. Seed-starting systems in a central place like an eating area are magical.

* grace from the garden

If you have stories of gardeners who have changed your life or the lives of others, please e-mail them to me at **deblandish@aol.com**. I'll post them on my Web site, **www.debralandwehrengle.com**, so we can continue to inspire one another.